What people are

Engaging with Muslin.

easy to read, understand, and apply to life. As a pastor, I am always looking for such resources to recommend to my church when it comes to making disciples of all nations. Klaassen does an outstanding job of providing a brief, highly practical, one-stop-shop on how we should view, understand, and minister to the Muslims around us. A wonderful resource for your church!

Dr. J. D. Payne, Pastor of Church Multiplication, The Church at Brook Hills, Birmingham, AL

This book will give anyone the confidence and the tools to befriend and share with the many Muslims that live in the US. I am excited to provide this book to the members of my church as we continue to reach out to Muslims at home and around the world.

Mike Wall, Associate Pastor of Global Kingdom Ministries, Henderson Hills Baptist Church, Edmond, OK

John is one of the most committed evangelists I know. His book is an essential resource for anyone concerned with sharing the good news with Muslims. Accessible and heartfelt. Practical and Passionate. A must read.

Dan DeWitt, Dean of Boyce College and author of Jesus or Nothing

Acknowledging the xenophobia, cultural distance, and religious ignorance that exists, John Klaassen aims to help Christians and whole churches understand more about the variety of Muslims living in the West, and to reach out to them with the gospel.

Erik Raymond, Pastor, Gospel Coalition blogger and author of *Gospel Shaped Outreach*

For some time now there has been a desperate need for a practical guide to assist Western pastors and church leaders in equipping their congregations for effective ministry among their Muslim neighbors. Filled with helpful illustrations, conversion stories, and questions for further reflection, *Engaging with Muslims* is the place to begin for those who are serious both about understanding their Muslim neighbors and reaching them with the gospel.

Dr J. Scott Bridger, Director of the Jenkins Center for the Christian Understanding of Islam

With the world coming to the doorsteps of North America, we no longer must cross oceans to tell Muslims about Jesus. They are beside us at work, school and in our neighborhoods. John Klaassen's book provides practical, biblical and compassionate wisdom on sharing the gospel with our Muslim friends. I pray that God will use this book to help Christians develop friendships with Muslims that will lead to opportunities to share Jesus.

Kevin Ezell, President, North American Mission Board

ENGAGING
with...

Muslims

understanding their world
sharing good news

John Klaassen

thegoodbook
COMPANY

Engaging with Muslims
© John Klaassen/The Good Book Company, 2015
Reprinted 2015

Published by:
The Good Book Company

Tel (US): 866 244 2165
Tel (UK): 0333 123 0880
Email (US): info@thegoodbook.com
Email (UK): info@thegoodbook.co.uk

Websites:
North America: www.thegoodbook.com
UK: www.thegoodbook.co.uk
Australia: www.thegoodbook.com.au
New Zealand: www.thegoodbook.co.nz

The stories on pages 33 and 104 are taken from *Jesus through Asian Eyes*. Ivan's story on page 69 is taken from www.christianityexplored.org. Used by kind permission.

ISBN: 9781909919112
Design by The Good Book Company / ninefootone creative
Printed in the UK

Also in this series:
- Engaging with Hindus
- Engaging with Atheists

Contents

Engaging with...

Preface

Christians have a wonderful message to tell the world. As the angel said at the birth of Jesus, it is "good news of great joy, *for all people*" (Luke 2 v 10). But sometimes we have been slow to take that message of forgiveness and new life to others.

Sometimes it's because we have become *distracted*. There are so many things that can push the need to tell others from its central place in our calling as individuals and churches. We get wrapped up in our own church issues, problems and politics. Or we get sidetracked by the very real needs of our broken and hurting world, and expend our energies dealing with the symptoms rather than the cause.

Sometimes it's because we have lacked *conviction*. We look at people who seem relatively happy or settled in their own beliefs, and just don't think Jesus is for them.

Or perhaps we have forgotten just how good the good news is, and how serious the consequences for those who enter eternity unforgiven.

But often it has been *fear* that has held us back from sharing the good news about Jesus. When we meet people whose culture, background or beliefs are so different from ours, we can draw back from speaking about our own faith because we are afraid of saying the wrong thing, unintentionally offending them, or getting into an unhelpful argument that leads nowhere.

This little series of books is designed to help with this last issue. We want to encourage Christian believers and whole churches to focus on our primary task of sharing the good news with the whole world. Each title aims to equip you with the understanding you need, so that you can build meaningful friendships with others from different backgrounds, and share the good news in a relevant and clear way.

It is our prayer that this book will help you do that with a neighbour, friend or work colleague who is an actively engaged Muslim, or who is from a Muslim background and culture. We pray that the result would be "great joy" as they understand that Jesus is good news for them.

Tim Thornborough
Series Editor

Introduction

I met him in a coffee shop near my house. He was from the Middle East, friendly as I expected, but nothing else went as planned. As we met together, I was astonished at how God had been working in his life.

Rachid's[1] father was a wealthy businessman who had studied outside his country and returned home a practical atheist. He raised his family to be wealthy but without religion, even though they lived in a predominately Muslim country.

Rachid grew up not knowing much about the *Qur'an* or prayer times, other than what he was taught in school. So when he went to college he was filled with questions. That was the time of the 9/11 attack in the US, and college campuses around the Middle East were alive with Islamic radicalization. But when Rachid asked what he thought were very reasonable questions, he was threatened for doubting Islam. He was called a *kafer* (infidel).

Because his father was wealthy, Rachid was able to travel. He visited the East to explore Hinduism and Buddhism, but he instinctively knew that there was only one God. As he continued his thinking, Rachid struggled to understand why Muslims kill one another and why they commit other immoral acts. As a result he began to study Christianity.

---

1 Not his real name—throughout this book names have been changed to protect the identity of people who may be in personal danger because they have professed faith in Christ.

In his country they have a saying: *"Eat with the Jews, sleep with the Christians."* You can eat with Jews as their food is *kosher* (equivalent to *halal*), but you can trust Christians. When you are asleep, they won't kill or hurt you. A Christian's moral compass is different. Rachid wanted to understand why.

Rachid was attacked and shot not long after returning from his travels because he questioned Islam and was intrigued by Christianity. The Muslims around him wanted him dead, so he fled to Jordan and managed to get refugee status to come to the West. While in Jordan, at an orientation briefing with other Muslims, he was told that when he got to America Christians would come to his house and give him things. He was advised to take what they gave him, but not listen to what they had to say. Secretly Rachid couldn't wait. He longed to hear the truth of the gospel. They also told him that if he ever went to a church he would be prohibited from entering—*"Americans just don't like Muslims,"* he was told.

When he arrived in the US he was placed in an apartment with other Muslims and he waited for the Christians to visit. They didn't come. He moved to a new place, unable to live with the other Muslim refugees, and waited longer. He walked past a local church but was afraid to go in because of what he had been told. It would be shameful to be asked to leave. Nine months passed without one Christian coming to his house as he had been promised.

He began to think God was angry with him so he prayed: *"God, just let someone come to my house; please don't be mad at me."* One day, not long after, he found a pamphlet on the ground near his door. It was for a free

Bible. He immediately wrote and asked for a Bible and more information about Christianity. They sent him the Bible but it was in English and his language wasn't very good. He was frustrated once again. This time he wrote and begged:

Just send me someone to tell me about Christianity. I will pay for them to come to me. I don't need anything; just send me someone.

The woman who received this message, by God's grace, happened to be the cousin of a pastor at my church. She called her cousin, her cousin called me, and I set up a time to meet with Rachid.

After meeting with me for six months and being at church with other believers, Rachid was baptized. What a glorious time of celebration we had that day, rejoicing with our church, who had grown to love him! Rachid continues to come, learn, serve and grow—a wonderful brother in Jesus.

In Matthew 9 v 37 Jesus tells us that:

the harvest is plentiful but the workers are few.

The harvest is plentiful? I worked in the Islamic world for over 18 years and it never felt plentiful, and yet there was a steady trickle of people coming to Christ. There were men and women who were ready to be harvested.

Over the course of the last few years the agency I was with discovered an amazing truth—**we don't see deci-**

sions for Jesus where we are not sharing the gospel! Ok, that's not so amazing; perhaps it's even a bit simplistic, but it's powerful none the less. If we are sharing the gospel, even in the hardest parts of the world, we see people come to Christ. We see men and women make Jesus Lord and Savior of their lives. However, if we aren't faithful in sharing the gospel, we don't see anyone come to faith. That must be what Jesus meant when he went on to say:

> Ask the Lord of the harvest, therefore, to send out workers into his harvest field. v 38

Sometimes we think this person or that people group or that religion is too hard to reach. When I share the gospel with Muslims, I understand God's promise to Hagar:

> And the angel of the LORD said to her,
> "Behold, you are pregnant
>   and shall bear a son.
> You shall call his name Ishmael,
>   because the LORD has listened to your affliction.
> He shall be a wild donkey of a man,
>   his hand against everyone
>   and everyone's hand against him,
> and he shall dwell over against all his kinsmen."
>
> *Genesis 16 v 11-12, ESV*

Arabs, the descendants of Ishmael, can be hard and argumentative, but sometimes they listen because God is working in them! God was working in Rachid, and he not only listened but also drank deeply from the well of living water that only Jesus could provide. The promise of Jesus wasn't that it would always be easy but that the harvest is plentiful! There are men and women waiting in their apartments and houses for you to come by and share Jesus with them! Pray the prayer to the Lord of the harvest—and then be willing to be the answer. If faith comes by hearing (and I believe that it does), someone must be telling! Might as well be you and me. The purpose of this book is to help you do just that—share your faith with a Muslim.

I need to make a truth very clear, from the beginning: **all Muslims are lost without Jesus.** I make no apologies for, and take no joy in, that statement. I have many Muslim friends who are lost, facing an eternity separated from God. The fact is Jesus said: "I am the way and the truth and the life. No one comes to the Father except through me" (John 14 v 6). As a result, I am convinced there is no other way to heaven but through Jesus Christ. Jesus cannot just be a prophet; he cannot just be a man: he must be God incarnate!

Only God himself could take our shame upon himself and pay the just penalty for our sin. Jesus was the propitiation for our sins; he satisfied the wrath of the holy God by dying on the cross for our sins. This truth bothers me! Jesus took on himself what was reserved for me. What I deserved Jesus suffered!

So I thank him deeply for what he has done and I serve him fervently because he calls me "son." Salvation was undeserved so I will not be ungrateful!

It is my prayer that as you read this book, you will

lose some of the very natural fears you might have about sharing the gospel with a Muslim friend, neighbor or work colleague. And that as you share that life-saving message, you will rejoice with heaven as the lost are found by Jesus.

Understanding Muslims

Chapter one

Who are these Muslims I meet every day?

I live in a city of about a million people. I can go for days or even months, without seeing a Muslim in certain parts of my city. But there are other places where I can see my Muslim fellow citizens every day. I can shop at their stores; I can visit in their homes; I can be their friend.

But to be their friend and really care about them—to love them as God loves them—I must know something about them. I need to ask questions; I need to learn about them. In the end though, my biggest question as a Christian is: how does the gospel intersect with their daily lives and beliefs? If I am their friend and I love them as a friend, then I must find those points of contact with the gospel and help them understand who Jesus really is.

So who are these Muslims I meet? What do they believe? How do I interact with them? Let me say, these are big life-learning questions that you will not find answers for by spending an hour or two reading a book. I am going to present to you some basic do's and don'ts, but in the past 20 plus years I have learned that everyone is different. Our Muslim friends come from different countries, cultures and ethnicities—and have different beliefs and practices. There is a common core of beliefs, but from that common core there are many different manifestations—from radicalized Islam like that of Al Qaida and Islamic State to more "charismatic" non-violent forms of Islam like Sufism—and then everything in between.

Most likely, your Muslim friend is somewhere in the middle. They are just trying to get by, raise a family, and keep their faith. The difficulties of doing these things may be compounded by the fact that they are in a strange place, surrounded by a new culture, and have lots of pressures pushing at them from many different directions.

It is not uncommon for first-generation families to send their daughters back to their home country, especially during those difficult teenage years, in order to protect the honor of the family. We have even seen mothers take their girls back home to "properly" educate them and find them husbands, often to the fury of their daughters! These mothers are willing to leave their husbands and sons in the West, travel back home and live in their country of origin until their daughters are raised and married. After the wedding they will return to their husbands and sons.

This brings us to some general principles and observations about Muslims, and how we approach being friends with them for the sake of the gospel.

1. All Muslims are different

For almost 20 years my wife and I worked in a primarily Sunni Islamic country where everyone pretty much believed the same things. Since moving back home we have had to adjust to all the different manifestations of Islam that a plural society has to offer.

The biggest difference lies in the fact that many of our friends are either **Sunni** or **Shi'ite** Muslims. This divide dates back to the sixth century and the death of Muhammad. The Shi'ites believe that Ali ben Talib, Muhammad's son-in-law, was the legitimate next leader of Islam. Ali, the husband of Fatimah (Muhammad's only daughter) had distinguished himself in his devotion and enthusiasm for the cause of Islam. He even claimed that Muhammad had endowed him with Muhammad's designation (*ilm*) and with special spiritual knowledge (*nass*). Ali claimed that he, like Muhammad, would be able to speak directly with God and continue to receive special revelation. However, Ali did not have the support of the majority. The people thought he was quick tempered, out of control and unreliable.

Abu Bakr, Muhammad's father-in-law, had also distinguished himself as a leader and wise man. After Muhammad's death the people wanted to confer divinity on him. Abu Bakr took charge and settled the issue by appearing before the crowd and saying: *"If anyone worships Muhammad, Muhammad is dead; but if anyone worships Allah, he [Allah] is alive and does not die."* He settled the issue and provided stability for the people. As a result, Abu Bakr was made the first *caliph* (successor of Muhammad). Ali's supporters, however, were not in favor of this choice and the seeds of division were sown. The Arabic word for this splinter was *shia,* and thus we have the origins of the *Shi'ites* (the minority) and the *Sunnis* (the majority).

One of the first questions to ask your Muslim friend is: *"Are you Shi'ite or Sunni?"* It is like being Catholic or Protestant; the chasm between the two is wide and deep. But just as all Catholics and Protestants call themselves Christians, so all Shi'ites and all Sunnis call themselves Muslims. You will not offend your friend by asking.

If you have friends from both groups, you will notice differences in their practice of Islam and especially in their celebrations. From that one major division there have been other minor splits and divisions. Today, within both the Shi'ite and the Sunni branches of Islam you will find a continuum of belief. There are radical fundamentalists who want to convert the world to Islam and there are liberal inclusivists who believe that everyone has a chance if they believe in the "one true God." There are also many cultural Muslims who have no idea about what they really believe; they just know they are Muslims and their children should only marry Muslims.

2. Don't speak disparagingly of Islam or Muhammad

When you are with your Muslim friends, *never speak disparagingly of Islam as a religion or of Muhammad.* No matter where your friends are on the continuum of Islamic belief and practice, all Muslims will instinctively defend Islam, and they will take it personally if you, as a Christian Westerner, speak in a hostile way about Islam or Muhammad. Many Christians want to debate or demonstrate the falsities or contradictions of Islam. We look for qur'anic texts that contradict one another or character flaws in the life of Muhammad, and bring those to our conversations. Sadly, the only thing that will do is drive a wedge between you and your friend.

They will not accept what you say for a number of reasons. First, unless you know qur'anic Arabic and can read from the original language, then your translation is flawed. In Islam the *Qur'an* is only authoritative in its original language. Any interpretation based on a translation will easily be dismissed as flawed, as it does not meet the standards of the Arabic language. The second reason is the rule of abrogation in the *Qur'an*. Abrogation is simply a rule of interpretation that states that what comes later supersedes or even nullifies what came before. There are three verses in the *Qur'an* that acknowledge and or justify abrogation.

When we cancel a message, or throw it into oblivion, we replace it with one better or one similar. Do you not know that God has power over all things?
Qur. 2:106

When we replace a message with another, and God knows best what he reveals, they say: You have made it up. Yet, most of them do not know.
Qur. 16:101

God abrogates or confirms whatsoever he will, for he has with him the Book of the Books. *Qur. 13:39*

Rather than explaining inconsistencies in the text, many Islamic jurists acknowledge the differences and accept that the later verses trump the earlier. As a result, if you try to argue and debate, you find yourself beating against a wall you cannot knock down. Better to find other ways to the heart of your friend.

Third, while it may be true that Muhammad demonstrated numerous character flaws, it would be pointless to highlight them since in Islamic thought he is never considered perfect anyway. He was a man—a very special man to the Muslim, but just a man. Their understanding of Muhammad would be like our understanding of King David in the Old Testament: a man chosen by God, a king, a prophet, and even a type of Christ—but full of flaws and sin. Muhammad never claimed to be God and never claimed to be perfect. After his death, some wanted to deify Muhammad, but that was not permitted. I have never met a Muslim that considers Muhammad to be more than a man. He is called *Rasool*, the spokesman for God; but just a man. Attacking the life of Muhammad seldom leads to fruitful conversations with Muslims.

3. Muslims believe in "one true God"

When you speak of *Allah* to a Muslim, the word carries connotations and meanings that as Christians we do not agree with. For example, *Allah* in Muslim thinking is distant and capricious—he does what he wants, saves who he wants to save—and is seldom seen as loving. *Allah* does not have a son; he is not trinitarian. To the Muslim, he is, however, all powerful, all knowing and everywhere. He is the Creator and Sustainer and will return one day. He is in control of all things and is to be submitted to. While we agree with some of the above, we cannot agree with everything. *Allah*, in Islamic theology, is not the God of Christianity.

Some Christians will talk to Muslims about *"Father"* or *"Father God"* in order to make clear that it is not *Allah* as they understand him that we worship. I think, however, that to use a non-Muslim name for God, and reject the term *Allah* is more than is necessary. Instead, redefine the name of God, *Allah*, and help your Muslim friend see and understand all that God truly is. *Allah* literally means "the God." In fact, if your friend is a first-generation immigrant from a Muslim country, he or she probably refers to God like that in English—"the God." It would be a literal translation of the Arabic. It's not bad grammar: just a true interpretation of the word. Therefore, using the word *Allah* gives you common ground and a common place to start.

We use the term "God" in English and it has all kinds of connotations in today's language that we don't like or believe. Westerners tend to see God as capricious, the old man in the sky, or the grandfather that accepts everyone or no one. None of these ideas are correct but we don't use another name for God when we speak of him; we just work to redefine the word for our friends so they understand who God really is. The name your Muslim friend uses for God is a great place to start a conversation telling him or her about your relationship with God, how you worship him and how you can know him.

4. Muslims have a sense of sin and a fear of God

I have never met a Muslim who, after reaching a clear understanding of what sin is, did not confess that he was indeed a sinner and that he had dishonored God in certain aspects of his life. While Islam does not teach original sin (that we are all born sinful), it does teach that we must not dishonor God with our lives. Islam also teaches that we must fear God. God is not near; he is not personal; he is to be feared and honored with one's life. The concept of God being a loving Father or the Savior of mankind does not exist in your Muslim friend's mind.

One of the earliest teachings of Muhammad was about judgment. The *Qur'an's* teachings on judgment are clear and sobering (20:102-127; 18:101-104; 23:105-115). At the appointed time, known only to God, a trumpet will sound and a general resurrection will follow.

All men and women have had two angels on their shoulders throughout their lives. One angel records their good deeds and the other angel their bad deeds. As the living and dead appear before God, they will be handed a book, and confronted with what they did in life. The wicked will receive their books in their left hand (in many Islamic cultures the left hand is unclean) and the righteous will hold their books in their right hand.

Judgment is based on sincerity and submission to the will of *Allah*. Only *Allah* knows the heart of the individual. Merely professing Islam is not enough to escape punishment; one must be genuine before God for a lifetime. *Allah* is considered to be "the most gracious" and "the most merciful" so he will probably forgive the most devout of their sins.

There is even some indication in the *Qur'an* that *Allah* will forgive the Christian and the Jew who sincerely lived by all the right obligations. But any claims of assurance of forgiveness would be considered presumptuous in Islam because that attitude would be like telling God what he must do. While God's mercy gives rise to optimism, no one genuinely has assurance of salvation.

This fact is important as you speak to Muslims in the West. I have heard more and more *imams* teaching that salvation is given by grace and that there is assurance of salvation. This teaching is actually foreign to Islam and is an over-contextualization to make Islam more palatable for the Western Christian. It is a false teaching in Islam; however, it is being told to non-Muslims in order to gain converts. When you hear it, don't be afraid to challenge the thought and ask where that is found in the *Qur'an*. Then explain how as a believer in Jesus you can have assurance of your salvation. Demonstrate the assurance you have in Jesus Christ with Scripture.

5. Presence is felt

This idea is very important to the majority of non-Westernized Muslims—*presence is felt*. In the West we like to think that what matters most in a relationship is quality time together. That idea is not really a concept for the majority of Muslims, especially those from the Middle East. For an Arab what matters is your presence: *time together*.

This idea is hard for most of us in the West. I tell my students that the most effective workers with Muslims are introverts. Introverts are happy with just a couple of friends; too many people wear them out. Generally, non-

Westernized Muslims want you to be *their* friend, not everyone's friend!

Practically, what this means is that *you must spend time with your friends*. You need to be in their homes and they need to be in your home. You may not be able to speak to them at first; you may have trouble communicating, but that is not as important as just being together. As Westerners we tend to be very task oriented. Your new friends are not as worried about tasks as about relationships. If you find that you cannot be with them as much as you or they might like, make sure you call them weekly. Even if the phone conversation is difficult, call and let them know you are thinking of them. Text them periodically through the day; this is the easiest thing to do. You may get some funny, unintelligible texts back, but it lets them know you are thinking of them and that you care about them.

This idea then brings us to an important concept related to space. Most cultures don't worry about personal space in the way we do in the Western world. The other day I was walking down the hall of my church with my Arab friend and I could tell that he wanted to hold my hand. He was just being expressive and wasn't thinking of personal space or where we were. I confess that on that particular day I created space as I wasn't sure people would understand what was happening!

Normally your friends will sit close to you; they want to feel your presence. This idea may make you a little uncomfortable at first but you will get used to it, and as your relationship deepens, you will be grateful to have such a good and close friend.

6. Show hospitality: *"Ask three times"*!

Sadly, most first-generation immigrants have never been invited into a Western home. Even second- and third-generation Muslims find it a rare experience. The answer is simple: *invite them to yours.*

There are a lot of reasons why we don't: we are busy and it is hard to have someone over that we still don't know very well and may be uncomfortable with. But, let me encourage you to invite them to your home and keep on inviting. Arab culture says that you need to ask three times before something is considered to be a genuine invitation. So don't expect your friends to accept your invitation the first time; you will need to push and keep on inviting. What will happen, most likely, is that they will say: "No, please come to my house." If that happens, take them up on the invitation! Relationships will be built and you will eventually get them into your home.

Sometimes, they are afraid to come to your home. One friend eventually confessed that they were afraid we might hurt them. They told some friends to be on the lookout just in case they didn't come home. We laugh at this thought with them now, but remember, they may be just as afraid as you are. *What should I wear? How should I act? What will they offer me to eat?*—these are all questions they are asking as well.

7. Accept hospitality

Most Muslims are very hospitable. If they invite you, don't hesitate to say yes. Typical Arab hospitality requires multiple invites, but they might as well get used to Western culture— you invite and it's a yes or no response. So when invited, accept the invitation. If they are refugees or students, they may not have much money; however, if they can, they will put out the food. I have been in homes and have been served what must have used up their entire monthly budget for food! Don't feel guilty and not eat. The insult of not eating will be greater than the hardship they might face.

At the same time, you don't have to eat until you are stuffed or have cleaned the plate. Leave food on your plate even when they are encouraging you to eat more. I can remember times, when we lived overseas, when the mother would literally pick up food and try to feed me or others in the room. You can easily say that you are full, say "thank you", smile, and say "Praise the Lord" or "*al hamdulillah*"("Thanks be to God" in Arabic). They will be happy and so will you. When you are in their house, you can ask to give thanks for the food, but pray *after* the meal not before—as that is the typical custom. More than anything, build relationships and enjoy the company on that first visit. If it goes well, you will have many more opportunities to share the gospel.

8. Honor and shame are very important concepts

Many Westerners do not understand the depth and subtlety of these ideas in Muslim cultures, which can seem alien to us. A couple of quick thoughts.

First, *"shame-based" cultures have strong connections to the world of the Bible.* As Westerners, we tend to be more "guilt based" in our cultural understanding. We do the right things because we fear punishment or look forward to the reward. Shame-based cultures primarily are concerned with maintaining honor and avoiding the humiliation of public shame. When you break the honor code, then shame comes to the family and it is not easily erased.

Anthropologists have suggested this cultural norm is pivotal to understanding Eastern cultures, and it can be seen from Morocco in the west to Japan in the east. Shame-based cultures tend toward a reliance on external sanctions for good behavior. Thus you will read of public floggings, stoning, or even suicides to protect the honor of the family. Shame cultures tend toward public humiliation or even the killing of a family member to restore honor in the family.

In the West, personal independence, even at an early age, is valued over mutual interdependence. As parents, we teach our children what is right and wrong. We expect those principles and guidelines to serve as benchmarks throughout their lives. Shame-based cultures, however, rely on public opinion and outward appearances to enforce their code of conduct. This has important implications for the way we share the gospel with Muslims.

Because in the West the majority of Christians come from guilt-based cultures, we think of Scripture in terms of guilt and innocence. Thus a typical Western gospel presentation places the emphasis on the guilt of the individual, our separation from God due to our sin, and the need for a personal decision to repent and follow Jesus— who bears our guilt on the cross. But this gospel explanation will seem alien to many Muslims for whom the key issue is shame and honor—not guilt.

The gospel is a wonderfully multi-faceted jewel, and in the Bible we are presented with a number of pictures of how we bear shame, and how honor can be restored to the follower of Jesus. These pictures speak powerfully to Muslims.

Honor and shame in Eden

In Genesis 2 v 29 God's word tells us that Adam and Eve were in the garden naked and unashamed—they felt no shame. In chapter three, after sin, they come to feel shame. Adam and Eve clothe themselves and hide from the presence of God. There is now shame and fear, seen by the fact that Adam later tells God: "I was afraid because I was naked; so I hid" (3 v 10).

So what does God do? First, he calls to them. Knowing full well what has just happened, he still calls to them and goes to them in their shame. Second, he punishes them for their disobedience. Sin has consequences and it is against God that we sin (Psalm 51). Third, he covers their shame. God takes the life of an animal and clothes Adam and Eve. He provides them with hope and expresses his love to them. What a picture! God cares for them in their shame and loves them in spite of all they have done. And he provides a means to honor them through sacrifice and a covering for their shame.

Honor and shame in Egypt

Another great example is found in the Exodus event. God allowed his people to fall into slavery. In any culture, at any time in history, being a slave is a position of shame and dishonor. No one wants to be a slave! The people of God, though, were just that—slaves to the Egyptians.

The beauty of the story for discussing with Muslims is

found in that God took slaves, the lowest of all people, and gave them a place of honor. God made them into a great nation and took away their shame. This act is the redemption story for us as well. We are slaves to sin. God took our shame upon himself on the cross so we could be given a place of honor. Paul writes in Romans 8:

> The Spirit you received does not make you slaves, so that you live in fear again; rather, the Spirit you received brought about your adoption to sonship. And by him we cry, "Abba, Father." The Spirit himself testifies with our spirit that we are God's children. Now if we are children, then we are heirs—heirs of God and co-heirs with Christ, if indeed we share in his sufferings in order that we may also share in his glory.
> *Romans 8 v 15-17*

No longer slaves: we were taken from a position of shame to a position of honor through Jesus Christ. Now we are adopted into the family of God with all rights, privileges and even the honor to suffer with the family when the time is right, for when one member of the family suffers so do all members of the family.

Most of Romans 8 speaks in terms of the fulfillment of the law; however, the shame and honor aspects of this passage will come through quite clearly to your Muslim friend.

9. Move past misconceptions

There are a lot of misconceptions and misinforma-tion that go around—on both sides. Muslims, especially non-Westernized ones, may think strange things about you; we often think strange things about them. Until you have asked questions and spent time with Muslims in your neighborhood, until you have befriended them and had them in your home, please withhold judgment. Even those who are covered from head to toe are probably not what you think! In some cases they may be wide open to the gospel, and we miss sharing with them because of our fears and misunderstandings. One of my favorite passages of Scripture is 2 Corinthians 5 v 16. Paul writes:

> So from now on we regard no one from a worldly point of view. Though we once regarded Christ in this way, we do so no longer.

Paul reminds us that we cannot look at people through "worldly" eyes! The world only sees what is on the outside—the *burqa* or the head scarf, or the beard and turban. But the gospel causes us to look at individuals as God sees them. Lost. In need of a Savior. Worth dying for! When we look at people through Jesus' eyes, it is as if the scales fall off and we see everything new.

Look at your neighbor, your co-worker, or the refugee down the street through Jesus' eyes. When you do, you will see a sinner, just like you, in need of a Savior.

I started this chapter by saying that to love your Muslim neighbor you must first know them. Enjoy the journey for it will not happen overnight. Learn; ask questions; watch what they do and then emulate them. When they come to your home and take off their shoes at the door, remember to do the same when you are in their home.

When you go to their house and they feed you, make sure you do the same when they come to your home. Have fun; love your neighbor; see what God does though you to reach your friend with the gospel!

Hilal's story

I am a Pushtun from the north-west frontier of Pakistan and while working as a waiter, I met with a Christian man every week for about two years to discuss religion. I was hoping he would become a Muslim. Although I was 24 years old, sometimes my way of thinking was immature, and I would only hear what appealed to my own biased opinion where Christianity was concerned.

But as I read the Bible, Jesus came across as someone more than a prophet when it came to miracles. He told the lame to get up and walk, he made the blind see, he raised the dead to life, fed 5,000 people with a few loaves and fish, and spoke with authority about the forgiveness of sins.

Jesus was always said to be *Al Masih*, the Messiah, in the *Qur'an*, but it did not explain what that meant and neither did any of the commentaries I read.

Gradually, a change began to take place within my heart and I began to look more seriously into what the Bible says someone must do to get right with God. When I learned about the need for a personal relationship with God, I finally decided to trust my life to Jesus for his forgiveness, and I received new life through the power of God's Holy Spirit.

Reflection

- What are you hoping to gain from reading this book?

- What fears do you have about speaking, and perhaps sharing the gospel, with someone from a Muslim background?

- Where do you come into contact with Muslims on a daily or occasional basis? What are the different possibilities for having a conversation and perhaps starting a friendship?

- What kinds of fears and false perceptions might a Muslim have about becoming friends with a Christian? How might you start to address some of those concerns?

Don't assume that all Muslims are radicalized fundamentalists—they are all different.

Do show interest in what kind of Muslim they are—Sunni or Shi'ite—and try to understand what that means for them in their belief and practice.

Don't speak disparagingly of Islam or Muhammad.

Don't be distant—accept invitations into their home, and invite them to yours.

Do be prepared to think differently about how to share the gospel with a Muslim—they see things in a very different way.

Don't rush to demand a response—it can take a long time for Muslims to understand and appreciate that the gospel is good news for them.

Chapter two

Pillars of Islam: beliefs and practises

Your Muslim neighbor may be Indonesian, North African, Middle Eastern, Central Asian or from the West, and you will find a wide variety of expressions in the practice of Islam originating from these different places. Some of your friends will be pious and others much more secular. However, all of them will be in agreement on the five pillars of Islam. These pillars are core to Islam, and while there may be some slight differences in meaning and the way in which they are practiced, these five pillars are relatively standard.

1. *Shahada* (the witness)

The first pillar is the *shahada*, or the witness of Islam:

I witness that there is no god but Allah, and that Muhammad is the messenger of Allah.

Repeating this creed is the entry point into Islam. More than once my friends would try and get me to repeat the *shahada,* as simple repetition will get you started on the "right path." Of course, a good Muslim will tell you that it must be repeated with the heart and cannot just be words that are uttered without meaning. Where I lived it was to be repeated three times to have effect and demonstrate loyalty to God and the prophet Muhammad. It is a serious commitment to repeat the *shahada* in the presence of a Muslim and should not be taken lightly.

Within this creed is the essence of Islamic theology. **First is the statement that there is no god but Allah.** The purpose is to remind the listener that polytheism (the worship of more than one god) is not to be tolerated.

According to Muslim tradition, Muhammad grew up in a polytheistic society where pilgrims came from great distances to Mecca to worship at the *Kaaba* (cube), dedicated to the main god of this shrine, Hubal. Built into the side of the *Kaaba* was a meteorite that was considered holy because it had fallen from heaven. Muhammad saw the fallacy of this practice, even though religious pilgrimages made Mecca a wealthy city. To this day pilgrimages are made to Mecca and the *Kaaba* is still central to Muslim worship; however, all the shrines and other deities were cast out. Now only *Allah* is to be worshiped there.

Second, Muhammad was the messenger or *Rasool* of God. Within Islam there are two types of prophet. One is simply a man of God who is recognized for his holy life. The second is one who delivers a specific message for God. Muhammad is one who had the privilege of receiving and then transmitting direct revelation from God. That direct revelation is the *Qur'an.*

Muslims believe the *Qur'an* is in and of itself holy. It

is, for the majority of Muslims, the very "word" of God. For this reason to desecrate the *Qur'an* by burning, tearing or writing in it is considered to be an abomination. Muslims treat it with the greatest respect and hold it in highest regard. Another book should never be placed on top of it; it should hold a place of honor in the home. It is not just another book or even just another revelation; it is the "word" of God.

For this reason Muslims will not understand why you treat your Bible as you do. An Arab friend was at church with me one day and someone laid their Bible on the floor. He was shocked that someone would treat God's word in such a disrespectful manner! And he was amazed that the Christian was surprised by his reaction! This event created a great opportunity to discuss the difference between how we understand the Bible and how a Muslim understands the *Qur'an*, but it also reminded me that when we spend time with a Muslim, we need to take great care to show respect and love for God's word—the Bible.

For a Muslim the *Qur'an* has always existed. It was not new when Muhammad began his revelations; it has always been. Because the *Qur'an* was given to Muhammad to be revealed to mankind, he has a special place in God's plan for the universe. Muhammad holds a very special place in the lives of Muslims. To denigrate or speak poorly of Muhammad is to speak against God's chosen one.

For this reason it is wise to not enter debates about Muhammad or the *Qur'an*. You can find things in the life of Muhammad that are disappointing and you can point out his sin (the prophets are not considered to be perfect and Muhammad never claimed to be without sin). And you can also find textual evidence of contradictions in the *Qur'an*. You may win the argument, but you will lose your friend. Such approaches will do more to alienate your friend than draw them closer to the gospel.

For a Muslim, simply the recitation of the *Qur'an* in its original Arabic is in and of itself a holy and worshipful event. Remember, the majority of Muslims can recite but cannot understand the Arabic used in the *Qur'an*. What is important for many is not the meaning but the sound and beauty of the original Arabic used in the time of Muhammad. For this reason there are no authoritative translations of the *Qur'an*. While it can be translated, it is only authoritative in its original Arabic.

2. *Salat* (prayers)

The second pillar is the *salat* or the ritual prayers. Prayers are to be done five times a day, every day. The prayers are done at sunrise (*al fajr*), the moment you can tell a white thread from a black one; at noon (*al dhuhr*); in the mid-afternoon (*al asr*); at sunset (*al maghrib*); and the last one an hour after sunset (*al isha'a*). They are best if done in the mosque; however, this is not mandatory.

A mosque can be any small room set aside for prayers. Shoes are to be taken off and the room dedicated to God and prayer. Many if not most mosques will have some type of minaret from which the call to prayer is made. Today, in many parts of the world, this call to prayer is done over a loudspeaker so that all might hear.

As a Muslim comes to pray, they must first participate in ceremonial washing. After this purification ritual, the man or woman will go into the mosque and say something like:

> I witness that there is no other God than the one God, and that He has no partner, and I testify that Muhammad is His servant and His messenger. O God, make me the fellow of those who have repented and of those who are pure.

He then will say: "God is great" (*Allahu akbar*), and repeat the *shahada*, the creed. Afterwards he recites a short prayer, an invocation against Satan, which is repeated three times. The first chapter of the *Qur'an* is quoted (*al Fatihah*):

> In the name of Allah, the Entirely Merciful, the Especially Merciful. [All] praise is [due] to Allah, Lord of the worlds—The Entirely Merciful, the Especially Merciful, Sovereign of the Day of Recompense. It is You we worship and You we ask for help. Guide us to the straight path—the path of those upon whom You have bestowed favor, not of those who have evoked [Your] anger or of those who are astray.[1]

If you read the first *sura* (chapter) of the *Qur'an*, you will note that it contains many of the words that are used when Muslims pray. It is important to understand that while the words may translate into your language, that does not mean that the definitions are the same. As with

---

1 Surat Al-Fatihah, http://quran.com/1

many other world religions and sects, it is important that you constantly define your terms as you speak with a Muslim. Make sure that they know that "grace" means unmerited favor, and that "mercy" is found in the justice of God and the death of Jesus on the cross.

As your friend continues to pray, he will then repeat: "God is great" (*Allahu akbar*), three more times and bow down. In this position he will say: "Glory to God, the master of the worlds." Standing he will then say: "God hears those who praise Him." He then prostrates himself three times while saying: "Glory to God the Lord most high." Kneeling, but lifting his head, he repeats: "God is great."

He will then pray: "O God, forgive me, have pity on me, direct me, preserve me, and make me great, strengthen my faith, and enrich me." Before bowing down a second time he will say: "God is great." Each prayer time comprises a certain number of these repetitions. Once finished, he can recite a chapter of the *Qur'an* and then offer a prayer of petition. He then turns his head to the right to greet the angel on his right recording his good deeds, and then he turns his head to the left to greet the angel on his left who records his evil deeds. He says: "Peace be on you, and on you peace."

When a Muslim prays in this form, at these specific times, he is completing his ritual obligations either in the mosque or outside the mosque. I have had friends who were in my home when the time came to pray, who asked if they could pray. I would lead them to a quiet room and allow them to pray there, offering them the opportunity to practice their religion but not to make a show of it in front of the other guests or my family.

Muslims cannot be interrupted during their prayers or they will have to start all over from the beginning, so if your friend is praying, please do not disturb him or her. There are some differences depending on where your friend is from or which branch of Islam is followed, but for the most part this is what it looks like.

Because Christians don't pray in such a ritualized form, your Muslim friend might think you don't pray at all. I do not encourage people to pray alongside their Muslim friends as I believe that this sends a message you don't want to convey. I would, however, encourage you to have fixed times of prayer if you are in a predominately Muslim community, or to share regularly with your friend how you pray and why you pray. Emphasize that Christian prayer is not done out of obligation but out of a desire to know and love the Father; and that we approach God not in fear, but knowing that our loving Father longs to give good gifts to his children.

Spontaneous prayer

Muslims will also pray spontaneously. This prayer is called the *dua* and is similar to how we pray. I encourage you to pray with your Muslim friend in this way. The way you pray, however, is important to your friend's understanding. After asking your friend if you can pray for them, don't fold your hands, close your eyes and bow your head to pray as they will not understand what you are doing. Instead, open your hands chest high with palms facing upward cupped together. Then with your eyes open, address God in heaven and pray for your friend and his or her family. Pray for God's protection and blessing in their lives, and mention any prayer requests they might have made.

Then close in the name of Jesus. Do not close in the name of God; always invoke Jesus' name at the end of your prayer. When I have offered to pray for someone, I have never had them refuse. While they sometimes question the end of my prayer, they are simply grateful to see that I am a man who prays. If you close your prayer in the name of God, while not formally wrong, it will convey the wrong message. When you close in Jesus' name, you associate Jesus to God in a way your Muslim friend does not understand. You want to establish that you are different and you view Jesus differently from your friend. By closing your prayer in this way, you will create opportunities to talk about how Jesus is different than all the prophets, and how he is in fact God.

3. Sawam (fasting)

The third pillar is *sawam* or fasting. According to Muslim tradition, Muhammad received the first of his revelations during the lunar month of Ramadan. Because Muslims operate on a lunar-month system, their calendar moves by about 12 to 15 days each year. So over the course of time, Ramadan will move from winter to summer and back again. During the month of Ramadan a Muslim is expected to fast from sunrise to sunset. They fast from all food, drink, tobacco products, sexual relations, and various forms of entertainment. They will not wear makeup or use perfumes and deodorant.

They can, however, eat and do what they like after the sun sets and until the sun comes up the next morning. It is said that more food is consumed during the month of Ramadan then at any other time of the year. The breaking of the fast is celebrated by the eating of a date and then, depending on the region, an assortment of foods that are consumed until late that night. One last meal is eaten before sunrise and many Muslims will then sleep as late as their jobs permit. During the summer months, Ramadan is hardest on the workers who must rise early and perhaps toil in the sun all day without being able to drink water to renew their strength.

Islam allows exceptions to the fasting rule in Ramadan if a woman is pregnant or nursing a child, if you are a child (most children fast a day or two in the beginning and slowly work their way to the full 30 days after puberty), or for adults who are advanced in age. There are also exceptions for those traveling or who are seriously ill. However, if time is "taken off" during Ramadan it must be made up later in the year. So you might find a friend fasting for a week later in the year to make up for what they missed during Ramadan.

Be aware that Ramadan is a time of great spiritual warfare and spiritual pride on the part of your friend. They are proud of the fact they are fasting and doing something to earn their way to heaven. At this time of the year they may often feel superior to everyone else. It can be an opportune time to talk about the purpose of fasting. However, if you never fast yourself, then your thoughts will fall on deaf ears. It is also a time of celebration, where you can break the fast with your friends, enjoy their company and have significant faith discussions.

The end of Ramadan ushers in the festival called *Eid al-Fitr,* which is three days of feasting and celebration where families gather in each other's homes and enjoy one another. Do not be afraid to use Ramadan to establish and deepen relationships with your Muslim friends. It can also be a time when they experience dreams and visions.

On or around the 27th night, the Night of Power is celebrated. Many Muslim scholars believe that it was on this night that Muhammad received his first revelation. The *Qur'an* describes this night as: "better than a thousand months" (Sura 97:3). Many Muslims will gather in the mosque and spend the entire night praying and seeking favor from God.

It should be noted that there is great debate as to when exactly this night is to be celebrated. However, for Muslims it is almost universally the most holy night of the year. Many believe that there are special angels who appear only on this night for the purpose of worship and to grant special requests of praying Muslims. On this particular night they are especially open to dreams and visions as they seek guidance and revelation.

Researchers suggest that about 80% of all new converts from Islam in South Asia come to faith because a dream or vision told them to seek the Christ. From North Africa to Southeast Asia many Muslim-background believers report some type of supernatural intervention in which God has revealed himself to them in the form of a dream or vision and told them to seek out someone, sometimes a specific someone, who would tell them the truth.

Years of encounters with believers and reading God's word have often preceded that vision or dream but not always. While not all Muslims have such an experience, many do, and the supernatural is an accepted part of everyday life.

I remember a young lady named Fatima, with whom my wife was spending a lot of time. She would come to a ladies' Bible study, primarily made up of some westerners and former Muslim women. Fatima was faithful but would leave as soon as the Bible study ended, full of fear and questions. Eventually however, she could no longer resist the call of Christ to not be afraid, and she came to faith and was baptized!

As her story unfolded, we learned that years before she had a dream. A man dressed in white told her to go to the city where we were living and find out about Jesus. Her good friend, who had converted from Islam, lived in the city so she started visiting and learned who Jesus was and why she should follow him. Fatima chose to follow Jesus as a result of Bible study and the testimony of several Muslim-background believing women. In general, people do not report coming to faith in their dream or vision but, like Cornelius in Acts 10, they are directed to someone who then shares the truth of the gospel with them.

So do not be afraid to ask the Father to send them dreams and visions pointing them to Christ!

4. Zakat (almsgiving)

The fourth pillar is *zakat* or almsgiving. While the *Qur'an* commands all believers to practice regular charity, there are no specific commands as to how that must be carried out. Muslim scholars have established that Sunnis are to give about 2.5% of their net income and Shi'ites are to give a much higher percentage. What I have found over time is that the percentage is not nearly as important as the act. Generosity is expected. One is to help those who are in need, especially family members.

When, as Christian believers, we show that we care for orphans, widows (James 1 v 27) and others in need around us, our faith rings loudly in the ears of our Muslim friends. Demonstrate that you care for others, that your faith means something in everyday life, and you will earn the admiration and trust of your Muslim friends.

5. *Hajj* (pilgrimage)

The last of the pillars, while expected if possible, is not mandatory. The *Hajj* or pilgrimage, is to be made once in a lifetime to Mecca. The month of *Hajj* is the last month of their lunar calendar. So, like Ramadan, it changes annually by about 12 to 15 days.

There are three primary holy cities in Islam: Mecca, Medina and Jerusalem. According to tradition, Muslims originally faced Jerusalem for their prayers, but after Muhammad's conflict with the Jews, he made Mecca the focal point of Muslim devotion. Medina is where Muhammad is buried and Jerusalem is where he reportedly ascended into heaven one night. The Dome of the Rock, in Jerusalem, marks the place where Muhammad made his temporary ascent. There are other holy places all over the world—the Shi'ites have several and many Islamic countries have specific locations that mark some special moment in history.

The recommendation to go to Mecca during the month of *Hajj* is for both men and women. Many Islamic countries have free lotteries whereby the working class can win a trip to Mecca once in their lifetime. Because of the sheer numbers of Muslims in the world today, people are encouraged to make only one trip. However, wealthier Muslims may travel many times for the *Hajj*, or they will go during another month for the *Umrah*—just like the *Hajj* but taken at another time of the year.

Once someone has done the *Hajj*, they take on the honorific title of *Hajj* or *Hajji*. This accomplishment is marked in different ways depending on the practices of the home country. Often, to show respect to an elder, the title will be used whether that person has done the *Hajj* or not.

I have met Muslims who have completed the *Hajj* and have been disappointed—it was not as life-changing as they expected. Many believe that once they have done the *Hajj*, they will be free from the bondage of sin, only for them to return and find no release in their conscience. What a precious message we have for them in Jesus Christ, who delivers us from this body of death!

These five pillars are to be practiced with great devotion and they outline the way that life is to be lived.

There are other practices—such as only eating that which is *halal* and abstaining from alcohol—which are typically universal but not absolute. There are many other rules and regulations that govern Islam—from dress to marriage to the raising of children—that will vary from country to country.

The key is to ask your friends **what they believe is necessary to honor God with their lives**, and then share what you believe and demonstrate with your life what it means to be a follower of Jesus Christ. They assume many things about you that are not true. Live a life worthy of emulation, a life worthy of the gospel, and you will challenge their view of what a Christian really is.

Reflection

- How do you feel about praying with a Muslim? Why could it be especially helpful for your friend?

- Have you ever fasted? How might it help you to understand Islam better and share the gospel?

- What questions might you ask a Muslim about their practice and beliefs that will build understanding between you?

- In what ways should you ask those questions that will build trust between you and give an opportunity to share the gospel?

Don't assume that you mean the same thing when you use words like "God," "grace" or "faith."

Do respect what they believe is necessary to honor God with their lives.

Don't take part in formal prayers with a Muslim.

Do offer to pray for and with Muslims in the name of Jesus.

Do be patient with your friends during Ramadan.

Do pray that God would reveal himself to your friend—perhaps even in a dream or vision.

Do show that you are living a generous, giving life out of love for Christ.

Engaging with Muslims

Chapter three

Four keys to fruitful engagement

It's important to have a basic overview of what Muslims believe. But it's equally important to understand the variety of beliefs and practices your friends may have.

Even in Protestant Christianity you will find a broad spectrum of expression and practice: different styles of worship, and different kinds of spirituality and doctrinal emphases. You will find the same in Islam.

I have a friend who gets out a block of clay that came from a holy site when he prays. When he does the *salat*, he bows down and puts his forehead on the clay, not on the ground. He still prays five times a day; he just does it a little differently than others.

In North Africa there are a lot of tombs associated with famous Muslim "saints," where local people go to pray. They hope that, by making a pilgrimage to that holy site, somehow God will bestow on them some special blessing or favor. As we said in the last chapter—take the opportunity to question and explore with your Muslim friend how they practice their faith. They will not be offended.

But the conversation must move on from understanding to engagement—from sharing your life to sharing your faith.

In this chapter I want to walk you through four keys of evangelism—all beginning with "P." I think that these four principles are invaluable when sharing your faith with a Muslim. I have seen the power of them in action and I believe that they are both biblical and foundational to sharing truth with anyone—especially with Muslims. They are: *prayer, presence, proclamation* and *persuasion*.

Think of them in pyramid form; we start with prayer at the base of the pyramid, and we slowly work up to persuasion. Note that persuasion is the smallest part of the pyramid, but it is also the pinnacle. The pyramid is not complete without all four pieces.

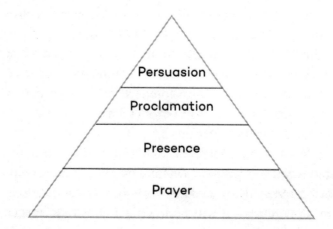

The prophet Jeremiah wrote to the exiles in Babylon. These people had been torn from everything they knew and were in a new land as strangers and aliens. Likewise, many of the Muslims you meet will be strangers and aliens in your home country. They are going through some serious changes and many of them cannot go home again. Jeremiah says to them:

This is what the LORD Almighty, the God of Israel, says to all those I carried into exile from Jerusalem to Babylon: *Jeremiah 29 v 4*

He reminds them that it was *God*, not Nebuchadnezzar, who took them into exile. Knowing that God is sovereign, even in the most difficult circumstances, changes everything. You may have gone for years without ever meeting a Muslim—but God, at this moment and time, has given you this contact, this connection.

This relationship is not an accident!

In the same way, your friend may have been born here to immigrant parents or descended from earlier generations, or come as a refugee, or arrived seeking a better life and job prospects. But in his sovereign mercy, God has brought them and their family near to you, so that they can hear the good news about Jesus who is the only hope for them eternally.

There is a neighborhood near our church that God has been filling with Iraqi refugees. There is absolutely no human reason for this to be happening. It is far from any other refugee center, and is inconvenient in a whole host of other ways. But, it *is* near our church. I drive by it every time I go to a meeting. Some people might see this as a threat locally. I do not. It is not an accident, but in God's mercy it is an opportunity for outreach with the gospel.

The Lord recently placed a Muslim-background believer in that neighborhood! This was not an accident either. God has a plan and we need to act in response to how we see that plan unfolding. *So what do we do?*

Jeremiah continues his letter:

> Also, seek the peace and prosperity of the city to which I have carried you into exile. Pray to the LORD for it, because if it prospers, you too will prosper. *Jeremiah 29 v 7*

Prayer

In verse 7 God tells his people to seek the peace or welfare of the city. The word for welfare in Hebrew is *shalom*—a word rich in biblical meaning which takes us back to the creation account.

> Adam and his wife were both naked, and they felt no shame. *Genesis 2 v 25*

Maybe you think this is a strange verse to be thinking about in relation to sharing the gospel with Muslims! But the point of the verse is not that they are naked, *but that there is no shame*: no hiding from God, and no hiding from one another—there is just *peace*. Perfect peace between Adam and Eve; perfect peace between Adam, Eve and creation; and most importantly, perfect peace between Adam, Eve, creation and the Creator! This is true *shalom*.

It's quite likely that every day your Muslim friend will leave their home and wish "peace" on everyone they meet. When they pray, they ask for peace for the angels on their shoulders. When they greet you, they say: "*Salaamu alikum*" (peace be on you). Your response is: "*Ualikum salaam*" (and on you peace). Your Muslim friend longs for peace but it cannot be found in works or a good life—and surely not in this world! It can, however, be found in Jesus. He is the only one who can offer peace. To know Jesus is to know peace! So Jeremiah very pointedly tells the Jews in exile that they are to seek the "peace" or "welfare" of the city.

How do they seek it? Jeremiah tells them to pray: "Pray to the LORD on [the city's] behalf." Prayer needs to be our starting point. We pray privately *for* our Muslim friends and we pray *with* our Muslim friends for the needs they have. We demonstrate we are people of prayer and that God answers our prayers in Jesus' name. Remember, if you have an opportunity to pray with a Muslim—*always pray in Jesus' name*. Even if a Muslim questions this, emphasize what Jesus taught us about prayer and asking in his name.

Earnestly seek God on behalf of your friends and encourage others to do the same.

Recently, I was with a dear older saint from my church. She shared with me that as she ages, there are a lot of things she can no longer do, but one thing she can do is pray. She asked that I share with her different needs in our ministry with Muslims so that she can be a prayer warrior on our behalf.

God has brought Muslims to our doorstep, sometimes from places we cannot easily access. We need to give ourselves to praying for them with an understanding that their eternity is on the line. They are condemned before God, as we all were without Jesus Christ (John 3 v 16-18). There can be no true peace in their lives because they do not know the Prince of Peace. So we pray.

What do we pray for?

When you are praying for your Muslim friends, you can ask for:

- opportunities to spend time with them
- opportunities to talk about Jesus with them
- opportunities to show kindness toward them
- wisdom to know how to answer their questions
- patience to wait for the Lord to work in their lives

But most of all, pray for the Holy Spirit to convict them of their sin, and convince them about Jesus the Savior.

We also need to hear what their needs are. Many still have family in their countries of origin that they long to see, or who are in danger, or ill. Pray that God would bring them comfort, work out travel plans, bring them hope, or help them through a difficult time. Follow up your prayers and ask about their situation, and look for what God is doing in their lives.

Finally, help your church become prayer partners with you in your informal contacts and friendships with Muslims, and with any organized ministry that is going on with the Muslims in your neighborhood. Bring this up in small groups and at other times when you pray together. Help your fellow church members to see an opportunity, not a threat. Help them to learn to pray *for* and not *against* Muslims!

Presence

We need to build relationships with all Muslims as the foundation of sharing the gospel with them. To do this, we need to be present in their lives. I hope you are already thinking about how you can do this for your existing friends. Remember the adage: Arabs like to "feel" your presence.

Occasional "quality time," like a lunch or a cup of coffee, may mean very little to them, although they probably understand you are busy. Like all of us, they too are trying to keep up with the Western lifestyle! Their kids will have many things to keep them busy—school, sports, music, dance, etc. They know that in the West you have to work hard and put in hours to move up in business.

With newly arrived Muslim men, there is a very narrow window of opportunity. It is best to start relationships as soon as you possibly can after their arrival in the country, because as soon as they can work, they will—and they will work hard! They will work as much as they can, as they seek to take care of their families and give them a good life. They often feel guilty for having pulled their loved ones away from their extended families, and are doing all they can to meet their needs.

There are many ways in which you can get involved as a church or an individual when the men arrive. Find ways to help them accomplish those goals. Help them with their English, their CVs and applications, and finding good jobs. When they first arrive, there is a lot to learn! Teach them how to work a thermostat in their homes, how to navigate the school system, and how to be involved in school. In many educational systems around the world, especially in war-torn areas, parental involvement is not as important as it is in the West. Teachers may send home notes with assignments. Help parents read those notes so they can understand what teachers want.

Sometimes it is helpful to attend a teacher/parent conference with your friend as they gain confidence in the language and culture. Your willingness to help will be a great testimony to your new friend. Many also need to register with a doctor and will need help to understand how the system works. This involvement in their everyday ordinary lives is a priceless investment.

Be sure to do the little things, like inviting them to your home and helping them feel that they have some sort of family in their new country. When you invite them to your home, please be patient and don't worry when they don't understand or don't want to eat your food. Buy your meat from a local Muslim butcher; in that way you can say that the meat is *halal*. This act will mean a great deal to them! Don't be upset if they don't eat much on their first visit to your home. Remember, everything is new and different for them—they are just as nervous as you are! Be patient, loving and kind; as time goes on they will eat more and be more comfortable.

On a practical note, depending on their country of origin and their background, they may not be accustomed to eating with a fork, knife and spoon. They may find spaghetti and other pastas very hard to eat—so please don't serve these on a first visit. Most people are accustomed to rice, potatoes, some vegetables and meat. The simpler you make the meal, the better it will be!

Sometimes when you invite your friend to your house, you will get an immediate invitation to go to theirs. When you go, take a simple gift like flowers or candy. When you eat together, eat what is placed before you, but don't eat everything on the table (or the floor, depending on their culture). Many cultures are embarrassed if everything is eaten, as it suggests they did not fix enough food and therefore have brought shame on themselves. Always leave food on your plate and be gracious.

If they are comfortable with you, they might have you sit on the floor in their house and eat from a common plate. This type of dinner arrangement can be quite challenging for the average Westerner who is not accustomed to sitting on the floor with their legs crossed. When you enter the house, you must take off your shoes, even though they may tell you not to. Try not to point the sole of your foot at anyone—it is considered rude. Do your best to sit comfortably. Laugh with them and just enjoy the new experience!

Lastly, eat with your right hand as much as possible. The left hand is considered dirty so if they ask you to pass something, please do so with your right hand, not your left, even if you are left-handed.

Depending on the country of origin, the family may or may not eat with you. Feel free to insist they sit with you, but they might be trying to honor you by not eating with you—much like the story of Abraham when the angels came to visit in Genesis 18. Abraham stood waiting to serve them as they ate. He did not eat with them—this would have been the custom of that day and is still the custom in many parts of the world.

When I was in Central Asia recently, we ate in the home of a village man. He served everything and while he sometimes sat for a few moments, he was continually getting up to make sure that his guests were well attended. As you become more a part of the family, those customs will change. Your goal is to eventually eat with the family as family!

Presence can be developed in lots of other ways—your goal is to spend time with your friends. Men, this must be done up front. As I said earlier, as soon as the men can work, they will! It will be harder to spend time with your friend once he starts working, so try to establish your relationship before that. Consistently calling, offering help, and—when possible—being with your friend will go a long way! Ask him to help you around the house as well. The way that houses are built, the electricity plugs and voltages, and lawn care may all be new experiences! Some men adapt quickly; others struggle.

Being present with women

The commitment to presence with women can be a lot more time-consuming. Muslim women are accustomed to having their sisters, sisters-in-law, and mothers around all the time. If they are new to your country and do not have relatives here, they will feel lonely and in need of family. It is a wonderful opportunity to be family to your friend, and you will see God do amazing things in their lives.

Your friend may also be seriously stressed! She may not want to be here, but has to be. Many refugee wives are here because their husbands worked for a foreign government, and terrorist groups have labeled them as traitors and marked them for death. In some cases these groups have attempted to kill them or other family members. They may have been near death or have seen the death of family members, and have had to escape the horrors of their home. This escape does not come without remorse, guilt and stress.

Many Christians want a "silver bullet" approach to evangelism—a simple argument or Bible verse that will knock over their friend's objections and result in their becoming a Christian. There is no such bullet. As you will see from the testimonies in this book, it takes time and often prolonged contact with a faithful, friendly, prayerful believer before most Muslims are impacted with the gospel message.

This kind of presence can be costly in time—but there are ways in which it can be made easier. Simply include your new friend in what you do. Are you going shopping? See if they will come with you. Are you at home with a baby? Invite them to spend the morning with you—they will not mind if you continue with your housework, and will feel included and part of the family.

Issues for men

Many immigrant husbands struggle because in their home country they were well-paid professionals—perhaps doctors, engineers or businessmen—and in some cases even members of a paramilitary force. But now they can't find work that equals what they once did. The only jobs available are warehouse or cleaning jobs that are mind-numbing to them!

People don't understand them, and their quality of life has dropped immensely. Now they live in apartment buildings where they once lived in villas. Now they can only afford a second-hand broken-down car, where they once drove a brand new luxury car. Not all refugees come from wealth, but don't be surprised to learn that many do. They feel guilty as they struggle to provide for their families, and they miss home.

In many cases they are angry they can't return, and feel betrayed by the governments in play—their government, your government, all governments! Don't worry; they can distinguish between the government's actions and the people who live under that government. But try not to defend or become defensive about government actions. Your new friend may have seen far more than you can imagine ever seeing or experiencing. Allow them to talk, and love them with grace and mercy.

For Muslim-background men who are more established there is another set of issues. They may have taken on Western dress, food, habits and values—and appear to have little connection with Islam—but still, under the surface, they consider themselves Muslim. They will have a very strong sense of loyalty to their family and traditions. The opportunities for relating with them may be broader—going to a sports event, hunting and fishing, or out to dinner—but many of the same principles will still apply.

Proclamation

Once you are accepted as a true friend, you have built a substantial bridge. You want to cross it! You want to get the gospel to your friend in ways that they can best understand. While the P pyramid is built from the bottom up, it is important to say that from the beginning you need to be sharing truth with your friend as much as you can. As you pray with them and as you testify to the things God has done, you will have started to build a foundation upon which you can share the truths of God's word.

Proclamation is the sharing of biblical truth, but it is rarely preaching. It might come in a lot of forms; for example, when you pray you also proclaim, because you pray in Jesus' name. However, we need to go further than just a prayer.

Let me encourage you, as soon as you possibly can, to start sharing biblical stories with your friends. If they can't read or speak English well, you can get a *Good News Bible* or *New International Reader's Version (NIRV)* and ask if they would like to read it with you. Or you can pick out Bible stories and tell them to your friends. Your overall goal here is to start talking about God and Jesus, and what they mean to you, and establish that you have a personal, loving relationship with God through Jesus.

For further ideas on which Bible passages to share and talk about, see Chapter 5.

This stage is not the time to try and find reasons to argue or debate—just lovingly bring up the Lord and talk about what he means to you. The point of proclamation is to start building a foundation of understanding. You will be talking about Jesus in a way that your friend has probably never experienced. It is at this point that you will want to share your personal testimony. Muslims generally like to talk about God, so it will feel perfectly natural to them in a way that many Western people are less comfortable with.

I need to mention that there are some Muslims who are very secular. In other words, they are Muslims in name only. They are Muslims because they originate from countries such as Iraq, Pakistan, Somalia or Egypt—or their parents do. They have seldom been to mosque and pray even less. In some ways they are more like your agnostic neighbor down the street who says he or she is a Christian but never attends church. Ivan's story on page 67 shows some typical features of this. However, although he was an atheist, his Muslim upbringing meant that he responded to the gospel with the same suspicions and doubts as a believing Muslim would. Do not let that be a barrier to you—just keep sharing with them!

The goal of proclamation is to declare the wonders of God and allow your friend either to accept or reject what you say. It could be that as you share the truths of God, your friends will no longer want to spend time with you. If that is the case, don't worry: they have not rejected you; they have rejected the Christ, the one who saves. It is not your job to save anyone! Your job is to share the wonderful story of the Christ.

Persuasion

Now you are at the top of the pyramid. You are deep in relationship and you have shared your story and God's story with your friends. They are listening to you and respect you.

Persuasion comes in many forms. It may mean getting deeply into discussions about assurance and forgiveness in Islam. It may involve detailed discussion to unravel some of the false ideas they may have about the Bible and Jesus. It will certainly involve showing how the gospel gives answers to the significant questions of life that we all have.

But at some stage it will come time to push. Paul wrote in 2 Corinthians 5 v 20:

> We are therefore Christ's ambassadors, as though God were making his appeal through us. We implore you on Christ's behalf: be reconciled to God.

To "implore" is to ask with passion, to encourage someone to be reconciled to God. Persuasion must always lead to that time in evangelism where you ask your friends to come to faith. You have talked about faith and you have explained to them that they need Jesus to be true believers—now is the time to "implore." If you have been diligent with the other P's, then your relationship should be such that you can share anything with your friends—you can disagree with them in a loving way. You love them and you spend time with them—it should be natural to implore them to follow the Christ!

I was with my father in the countryside in North Africa. I brought my dad to share the gospel with my Muslim friend. My friend was my age and I wanted him to hear about Jesus from a man who was older than us. So my dad shared with him and I translated into Arabic. After a while, I got tired of translating and we just started talking about faith. Soon our voices were raised and we were speaking quickly and probably a little too loudly. My dad leaned over and asked what we were saying.

"I am telling him that if he doesn't submit to and trust in Jesus, then he cannot be saved and he will go to hell when he dies."

"And what is he saying in return?"

"Well, he's telling me that I must submit to Allah and the prophet Muhammad or I will burn in hell myself."

To this my father responded: *"Well, you'd better cool it or he might try and send us there himself while we sleep tonight."*

I told my dad that this would never happen because we were guests, and more importantly, he was my friend. He was like a brother to me! I could tell him anything I wanted because he knew it came from my heart.

Persuasion can only happen when you are in a deep relationship that permits you to say what needs to be said. Prior to that deep relationship it is proclamation. Proclamation might be saying there is heaven and hell. It might be a clear presentation of the gospel. It might be sitting and reading the Bible with them, and allowing the stories of the Bible to make their own impact. Indeed, it should be your aim to make a full presentation of the gospel prior to any attempt at persuasion. However, persuasion is that moment when you plead with your friend. In Romans 9 v 1-3 Paul explains the depth of love he had for his fellow Jews:

> I speak the truth in Christ—I am not lying, my conscience confirms it through the Holy Spirit—I have great sorrow and unceasing anguish in my heart.

For I could wish that I myself were cursed and cut off from Christ for the sake of my people, those of my own race.

Can you believe he wrote that? That is passion; that is heart; that is love for lost people. Sometimes when I read those words, I feel great conviction over my lack of passion for lost people! Lord, may I love in just such a way. Persuasion takes love! When I tell my friend that he might go to hell over his lostness, I do not say that with joy, but instead with a broken heart for his lost state! May you find such passion in your persuasion!

The four P pyramid, remember, is a pyramid. It all starts with *prayer*—a burden for lost people, a burden for Muslims. In today's world of Islamist terrorist groups like Islamic State and *Al Qaida* it is hard to have that burden. When you find yourself feeling that way, don't be afraid to ask God to change your heart. Don't forget, he did not just die for you but for every sinner. God has no enemies he has not shown love to through the cross of Christ, and neither should you have enemies to whom you show no love.

Presence is next. Presence equals *time*—plain and simple. Find ways to spend time with your friends, to genuinely love your neighbor.

Then *proclamation*—start sharing the truth of the gospel. Share with your life, your works and your words. Tell your friends biblical stories; talk to them about how God has changed your life; don't be afraid to share the truth!

Now the foundation has been built, ***persuade***, encourage, implore your friend to trust in Jesus. Not because they are projects to be completed, but because they are humans in need of a Savior.

Don't underestimate the amount of time that might be involved in forming a proper friendship with a Muslim man, woman or family.

Don't be surprised if Muslims are cautious and suspicious of your motives. Don't treat them as "gospel fodder" to be dropped if they do not seem to be responding. "Let love be genuine." (Romans 12 v 9)

Do find out what their background is, and what worries and concerns they may have about friends and family in their countries of origin.

Don't be too hasty to jump in with the gospel.

Do share naturally about your faith in God from the very beginning.

Ivan's story

I was born in Iraq. I come from a mixed religious and cultural family—my dad is an Arab Muslim, but kind of a liberal Muslim, and my mum is Armenian, so she's culturally Christian. My dad had to flee Iraq because of the political problems with Saddam Hussein, so when I was a teenager I was sent to study on my own in Czechoslovakia. I lived there for eight years, and I embraced materialistic philosophy and became an atheist and communist.

To me, religion was basically a waste of time. I had no respect for religion because I thought it was all made up of fantasies and myths: that people twisted things to suit their agendas and they created systems of belief to manipulate weak and disillusioned people.

One day I got very angry and lost my temper with the woman I loved at that time, and the relationship ended—she just left me. And I just couldn't face that loss; I just couldn't deal with it. And that was amazing to me because I had thought I was able to go through life and nothing would faze me—that I could get through any problems. But the reality was that it uncovered my weakness, and I realized that all this inner strength that I believed in was nothing, was worthless.

And I suddenly realized: "*I am to be pitied like those people I pitied before.*"

I started reading the Bible from the book of Genesis, and later on I started to go to church to hear sermons explaining what the Bible is. And there was this *Christianity Explored* course, so I decided to join it.

Middle Eastern people like me always have a suspicious mind; we always think there's something not true in what people say. So I tried to ask all sorts of questions to find out if the leaders on my table would tell me the truth, or if they would try to manipulate me or twist things or soften things up so I would think: *"Actually, it's not so bad."*

I discovered that they were just plainly explaining what the Bible was saying.

And also I just started to realize who the person of Jesus Christ really was. I had had all sorts of ideas about him before; but I started reading his words, hearing the stories he told, and understanding what he did—and he blew me away. I thought: *"This is the person I always wanted to be like in my life. I never thought there was anyone who could be like this!"* I was totally blown away by his integrity, and the things he did and said.

It was when I went on a day away, which is part of the course, that I just came to the conclusion that I could not keep denying the truth about Christ and who he is. And I just said: *"That's it—I don't know what this is going to do to me, but I trust you, Jesus, and I'm ready to follow you wherever you take me."* And that was it.

Life now has no meaning without Jesus Christ. It's like a journey I am on with him—with the one Person who we were created for. I can go walking all my life knowing that in the highs and the lows, in the sorrows and the joys, he is walking with me, never leaving me or abandoning me.

Not just that: this relationship doesn't end with my death—actually, it carries on forever. And that's what I can look forward to—that's what life is all about—not just now but also forever. I will enjoy that loving relationship with Jesus Christ forever.

Although many Muslims will seem to be convinced in their faith, this can often mask a deep-seated doubt. Notice from this story the importance of patient, but persistent encouragement, love, and a warm family atmosphere—all of which nurtured faith in Christ.

Shwan's story

I grew up in Sulaymaniyah, a city in southern Kurdistan. I was brought up in a Muslim family and moved to Europe because I wanted to go on an adventure. While I called myself a Muslim, deep down in my heart I knew I wasn't. At points I still tried to act like a good Muslim. If people offered me pork, for example, I would refuse. In Islam the hope is that you will go to heaven if you follow all the rules and regulations—if you pray five times a day, ceremonially clean yourself and go to the mosque. But there is no certainty. At the end of the day you could do all these things and still not get into heaven.

I started looking to other things to give me happiness. I tried many things, like going out drinking with friends. But although they made me feel happy for a short time, it would never last. I wanted to be happy all the time, no matter what my circumstances.

As I was walking through town one day a man gave me a leaflet about Christianity. I immediately put the leaflet in the bin. The next day I saw the man again. He stopped me and asked if I wanted to come to church. I told him that I wasn't a religious man and that church was for religious people. He said I didn't need to be religious to come to church.

Before I knew it he had persuaded me to come to a prayer meeting that night. One of the members of the church kindly picked me up. I remember sitting at the back of the church building. One of the leaders came up to me and started talking to me.

He was very warm and encouraged me to sit at the front. Afterwards they gave me a Bible and asked me to come along next Sunday to the service.

Next Sunday I decided to go. I was late and had to take a taxi. I was struck by how kind people were. I asked myself: *"Why are people doing this?"* I started going along to Bible studies with families even though my English, at that point, wasn't great. After four months I respected Jesus but I didn't trust in him. One of the leaders advised me to pray and ask God to help me believe in him, so I tried.

For a time I thought Jesus was only for the highly-educated. But I believe Jesus spoke to me and said: *"Come to me, I will love you as much as I love them."* I found true peace and happiness when I turned to Jesus as Lord and Savior. In 2008 the leaders of the church asked if I wanted to be baptised.

I didn't even know what baptism was! I wanted to invite people so five or six of my Kurdish friends came to see me baptized. When my Kurdish friends asked me why I kept on going to Bible studies and church services, I told them I felt like a beggar who had found food and now I wanted to tell everyone about where they could find it too.

Chapter four

Bridges to the gospel

I am flying over the mountains out of Central Asia. I just spent a week with some friends who are working to engage with Muslims in this part of the world. What an exciting thing it was to be with them and see their lives up close.

We went to a village where my friends had carried out a project to bring clean water to the village—they had developed deep relationships with the people there. The gospel was shared as a result. I am reminded that with Muslims, almost anywhere in the world, if the relationship is deep, truth is always welcome. So what are some bridges—stories and methods of evangelism—that you can use with your Muslim friend?

We have talked about the need for prayer, presence, proclamation and persuasion with your friends. What are some practical entry points to practice proclamation with them?

Personal testimony and biblical stories

One of the first entry points is the use of your personal testimony and a biblical story. I was once with a Muslim who was the head of his village, and appeared to be a sincere and good man. When I find myself in a situation like this, I always share the story of Cornelius from Acts 10.

Cornelius was a good and honorable man: he prayed, he gave to the poor, he worshiped one God and he had a great reputation. The Jews held him in high esteem for all the things he did—even though he was a Roman centurion. One day God sent an angel to speak to Cornelius, who told him to have no fear because God had heard his prayers. God told him to send for Peter. He told him where to go and find him. After the vision Cornelius sent some of his most trusted men for Peter. By the time they arrived where Peter was staying, God had prepared Peter through his own vision to speak to Cornelius. Peter was ready to share the good news about Jesus with Cornelius.

I emphasize to my friends that Cornelius was a good man: he prayed, he gave to the poor and he had a great reputation. But that did not make him right with God. He lacked one thing: *Jesus*. I have now anchored my own personal story in Scripture. From here I move on to my personal experience.

Just as Cornelius needed Jesus, I needed Jesus. I explain that I was a good person—I did the right things, I prayed—but I could not get to God through all my good works. I was separated from God because of the bad things I had done in my life. I had brought shame to God as a result of living for myself instead of honoring him with my life. I needed Jesus to restore me—just as Cornelius needed

Jesus, and just as my Muslim friend needs Jesus.

Depending on how that has gone, I will often then quote John 14 v 6. Jesus said he is: "the way and the truth and the life. No one comes to the Father except through [him]." Cornelius could not come to the Father on the basis of his good deeds. I could not come to the Father on the basis of my works; neither can your Muslim friend come to the Father on the basis of their works.

Using a biblical story adds power to your testimony. One thing you will discover is that many Muslims also have some form of personal testimony. If you only talk about how God changed your life, then you have done a good thing; but they might do the same thing in return. By using a biblical story, you can return to the Bible and talk about what it says, not about what you think or what they think, not about what has happened to you or has happened to them. Your goal is to get to the Bible as quickly as you can—because the Holy Spirit loves to use the words of the Bible to bring conviction and faith to people. The Bible will open up the real differences between Islam and Christianity.

When my wife shares her testimony, mostly with other women, she uses the story of Hagar. When Hagar was chased away from Abraham by Sarah, God came to her in the desert and spoke to her. He made promises to her about her descendants. For a Muslim lady to hear that God speaks to a woman is a big thing!

My wife then talks about how God came to her and spoke to her through God's word, offering her salvation through Jesus Christ. Using the story of Hagar is a great way to introduce the Bible into your conversation with

Now read it, read it again, and read it one more time. Then pray again and ask the Father to help you take what might be a long story and turn it into a story that you can share in just a minute or two.

Remember this rule: for the sake of brevity or clarity it is *okay to take out*, but it is *bad to add*. Please do not add to the story; don't add your thoughts or what you heard in a sermon. Let God's word speak for itself. When I tell a biblical story, if I have a Bible in front of me I will open it and say: *"This is a story from God's word."* Then when I finish the story, I will simply close the Bible and continue with my story. If you don't have a Bible, put verbal markers around the story by saying to start: *"This is a story from God's word,"* and close with: *"This was a story from God's word."* Set the story apart so that you can return to it later and have them read the story if they are literate, or learn it by memory if they are non-literate.

For example, when I tell the story of Cornelius, I leave out the section about Peter and his dream. It adds a lot of detail that I don't need on that particular day. I want to focus on Cornelius, not Peter. Later I will come back to the story of Peter and say something like: *"Remember how I told you Peter also had a vision? Well, this was his vision".* Then I tell them that part of the story. Was I wrong to not include it the first time? I don't think so—it would only have made the story much longer and added details that I needed to add only later. So think and pray through your story and decide what to leave out, but remember never to add anything to God's word.

Talking about *salaam*

As you practice proclamation, you are looking for entry points. Another entry point is to talk about *salaam* or peace. Every day your friends will wish for peace in the lives of the people they meet. Many will even greet the angels they believe to be on their shoulders with: *"Al-salaamu alaykum."*

We know that in the Garden of Eden there was perfect peace. Sin, however, broke that peace. Now there is war; there is enmity with God; there is shame. We are separated from God by our sin. I have never met a Muslim who will not admit to having sin in their lives, once we carefully define what sin is. They will also eventually admit that there is no guarantee that they can do enough good works to get to heaven. Their only hope is the mercy of God. However, the average Muslim must admit there is no real hope because in the end God does what he wants on any given day. He will determine your destiny.

Genuine *salaam* or peace with God involves four elements of life. The first is our relationship to God. This relationship is primary. Without it, there is no peace in any other aspect of life. One of the best authors that I know on this subject is Bryant Meyers in his book *Walking with the Poor*. Meyers does an excellent job of describing the nuances of what it means to be impoverished due to our lack of *salaam* or *shalom*. Our sin has separated us from God and there is no return. We have dishonored God because of our sin. Honor and shame are fundamental to the majority of Muslims. As you discuss this subject, help them understand that our sin dishonors God; it brings shame upon us because we do not measure up to the perfect nature of God himself. As our Creator, God expects us to live in right relationship to him, and always to do the right things. God is holy and he cannot allow someone who has dishonored him into his presence. Instead, he must be holy and just and punish those who have dishonored him. As such, we are all separated from God and facing judgment that is both deserved and earned by us.

In an honor-and-shame society there is no such thing as "mercy," which would allow the one who has brought shame to be restored. Instead, a penalty must be paid; often a blood sacrifice must be offered. Then, and only then, can honor be restored. As strange as it may seem to us, this is why a father can justify taking the life of a son or daughter who has brought shame on the family, even though it is illegal and abhorrent. In his mind, however, honor can *only* be restored by that blood sacrifice.

God too requires a blood sacrifice, which is why in Paul's letter to the Philippians he writes that Jesus endured the "shame" of the cross. He doesn't mean that the cross was embarrassing—in the way that we usually use the word "shame." Rather, Paul is referring to the way the shame of us all bore down on Jesus so that honor could be restored.

Your Muslim friend will understand this. Honor can only be restored by someone who takes on the dishonor to restore honor to the family. Jesus bore our shame, the Bible says, so we can be restored to the family. What wonderful news for your Muslim friend! Peace only comes when honor has been restored, and it is only restored in the wonderful work of Jesus on the cross. Normally a Muslim will argue with you that Jesus could not have died on the cross, because they have no framework for understanding Jesus' death. This, however, provides them with an understanding as to why Jesus had to die.

Once honor has been restored with God, then it can also be restored between fellow men. Now we can love our neighbor as Jesus commanded us—this is why you do good works and care for those around you. Remember what we talked about with presence? This work of God is what makes you different from everyone around you. You can even love your enemy. This concept bothers Muslims deeply. How can one love his or her enemy?

Eid al-Adha

There are other entry points to getting to the gospel, but I only want to mention one more. The story of Abraham and the sacrifice of his son Isaac is in Genesis 22.

Every year your friend will celebrate the *Eid al-Adha* also known as "The Greater *Eid.*" It is even more important than *Eid al Fitr*, which ends Ramadan. It is a time in which they remember the faith of Abraham as he went to sacrifice his son. In the Old Testament, this story is, of course, about Isaac, but in the *Qur'an*, the son is identified as Ishmael. This festival is like Christmas to you and me. New clothes are purchased and they celebrate for three to seven days. In the West your friends may have to work on those days, but they will do everything in their power to take them off. If you are in a position of influence, encourage your supervisor to let them off or give them the time off yourself, just as you would appreciate having time off for Christmas.

If you celebrate with them—often you will be invited to their homes—ask them to tell you the story of the sacrifice. At this point it is not important to worry about the name of the son being offered as a sacrifice. Eventually you will want to make sure your friend knows what the Bible says. However, during their celebration is not the time to argue.

It is, however, the time to celebrate the substitutionary atonement of the Lamb. What better Old Testament story to demonstrate the fact that the son was condemned to die? Abraham was ready to take his life, but then God gave a substitute! Honestly, your friend has probably not thought a lot about that part of the story. When he or she tells the story, they will probably talk about the faith of Abraham and how we too need that kind of faith. However, you can bring out the other aspect of the story and talk to them about the lamb that took the place of the son condemned to die.

You can bring out the fact that Jesus took your place as you were also condemned to die due to the nature of your sin; you had dishonored God with your life. But God provided a Substitute, one who lived a perfect life, who could take our shame and restore our honor as no one else ever could. I believe this is one of those stories that God provided for us to share with Muslims. This feast is important and they love the story. Help them see the whole story; don't be afraid to share the beauty of the Lamb!

Using the *Qur'an*

If you have done much reading on evangelism to Muslims, at this point you might be asking about whether it is legitimate to use the *Qur'an* in evangelism. I can only share with you what I have seen and experienced.

Some Christians have developed a way of evangelism which seeks to explain the gospel from the words of the *Qur'an*. One version of this is called "the camel method," —and some have argued that it is an effective bridge to the gospel. There is a whole chapter in the *Qur'an* called *Miriam* and it talks about Mary the mother of Jesus. The chapter talks about Jesus' virgin birth and elevates him above all others. It talks about him being the "word" of God. Islam also suggests that Jesus is with God now and that he will return one day to judge the living and the dead. There are a lot of bridges here that can potentially be used.

Let me say something about a bridge: no one camps out on a bridge. If you choose to use the *Qur'an* as a bridge, let me encourage you to get off it as quickly as you can. For example, Muslims, if they choose to be combative, will suggest that you believe God had relations with Mary and Jesus was born as a result. This thought is vulgar to me and I won't hesitate to point that out. I will then point out that the *Qur'an* says the same thing as the Gospels (*Injil*) say about the virgin birth. But then I move on and try and return to the Bible.

Let me remind you of three things if you are going to use the *Qur'an* in evangelism and apologetics with a Muslim.

- First, realize that your friend might not know much about the *Qur'an*. Since it is only authoritative in Arabic (the Arabic of the time of Muhammed), they might not understand it even if they can quote it. They were never taught to study it, but only memorize it. So they may or may not believe you when you say the *Qur'an* says this or that.

- **Second, since the *Qur'an* is only authoritative in the original Arabic, your translation is always considered to be faulty.** So the argument can always be made that you don't really understand what it says.

- **Third, remember the law of abrogation:** what comes after takes precedence over what comes first. In the beginning Muhammad sought to have good relations with both the Christians and the Jews; however, that changed over time. In the beginning, the holy books were the *Torah* (the Old Testament), *Zabur* (the Psalms and Proverbs), *Injil* (the Gospels) and the *Qur'an*. Over time it was said that the *Torah*, *Zabur* and *Injil* were corrupted and not to be trusted. What you read may in fact be corrected by a surah later in the *Qur'an* or some other writing.

For these reasons I try and stick just to the word of God, the Bible, and I don't worry a lot about the *Qur'an*. There are others who disagree with me. They have valid points and are quite capable when using the *Qur'an*.

Many Muslim-background believers are quite effective when using the *Qur'an* and comparing it with the Bible. They can often use the *Qur'an* in ways that you and I cannot. There are other Western apologists that are also quite capable in using the *Qur'an*. I would suggest that you pray and seek the Father as to how much of the *Qur'an* you want to try to learn and use. My encouragement is to immerse yourself in God's word and use it to demonstrate truth.

Sometimes when we tell a story that is common to both the *Qur'an* and the Bible, our Muslim friend will want to tell their version as well. I will often, out of common courtesy, allow them to tell their version either before or after I tell the biblical version. When they tell their version, I will listen and not interrupt, and then insist they do the same. We then compare and contrast the stories, always asking for application at the end. What does this story teach us about God, and how must it change our lives?

Life under God: life with the Father

Islam teaches you that God is involved in every aspect of your life. For a Muslim, whatever happens was written by God and predetermined. What that means for you is that you can approach life with your Muslim friend and always talk about God. Every aspect of their lives is centered around God and his plan for them, which does not sound so different from what a Christian would say.

The biggest difference is the *nature* of the relationship. A Muslim is subject to a God who is *intricately* involved in life. But a Christian lives a life with God, who is *intimately* involved as your Father with your life—and you are his son or daughter. What a difference that should make in the way we live! We can have a joy and confidence in life that is unknown to a Muslim, who lives constantly without the assurance of forgiveness. So the challenge for us is to live that life and show what it means to know peace with God now. Talk about God and what he is doing in your life and in the world. Be a spiritual rock that lives a life worthy of the gospel.

Make straight the path

Now you are sharing biblical truth with your friend, and you are living your life in such a way that the gospel is demonstrated; they are seeing your struggles, pains and how you find solace in Jesus. You pray to him and honor him in every aspect of your life. *Surely*, you might think, *I will see my friend come to faith.* If only that were true!

I wish I could share with you some silver bullet that works every time and will bring great conviction to your friend and will humble them to the point of giving their lives to Jesus, but you know it doesn't work like that. The amazing thing about God is that he is the one who converts; it is not you, not your words and not your winning personality. I think that is what I like most about evangelism.

My job is to tell the story, share the good news, and make straight the path. John the Baptist said that was his job, as he quoted Isaiah and said he was to:

...make straight the way for the Lord. *John 1 v 23*

The picture in Isaiah was of the coming of a king. When I lived in a country that had a king, every once in a while he would make his rounds and come to my town. It was always a huge event. I remember one time; they had just finished construction of an Islamic library near my house. In front of the library there was a nice little park that hadn't been touched by a gardener in years. You could still see the beauty that once was, but now it was in disarray. Where I lived they liked to paint the sides of the road to tell you where you could park and where it was prohibited. They hadn't been painted in years.

About a month before the king was due to inaugurate the library, things started to change. An army of gardeners came and tore out the weeds and fixed up the grass in the park. Painters came and painted the curbs. They even repaved the street the king would travel down to visit the library. The day of his arrival, the place was transformed: flowers were planted, holes were filled in, streets were swept, and everything looked amazing. The way was made ready for the king.

In our outreach we are called to do much the same. We are called to make ready the way for the Lord; to make his paths straight and smooth. This means we are to share the gospel in ways our friends can understand. Answer their questions as best we can. Get to work on their biases and presuppositions as to what a "real" Christian is. Allow room for the Holy Spirit to work in the life of our friends. We are never called to convert them, convince them, or change them—only to share truth with them in love, and make straight the path of the Lord.

Making straight the path is not insisting that they dress and look like us. It is not telling them that they have to change their culture, eat pork or drink alcohol. In fact, our goal should be that on the outside they look very much the same when they come to Christ. They don't need to dress like us, eat like us, or act like us to come to faith.

I learned a long time ago that worship in a church

placed in a culture different from mine should feel very different. Their culture, cultural preferences and worship styles will be different from mine. There is nothing wrong with that! There are universal truths of the Christian faith, but there is no universal *style* to Christian believing, belonging and worshiping.

In fact our end goal for a first-generation church plant of Muslim-background believers should be one that worships in their heart language, sings in their own cultural style, and preaches and teaches using their preferred methods. It should be very different and might not be comfortable for me, but that isn't my goal, is it? My goal, my heart, is to see worshiping Muslim-background believers, whether Westerners or first-generation immigrants, joyfully loving Jesus.

Reflection

- Think about how you came to faith in Christ. What story from the Bible can you explicitly link your story with for your Muslim friends?

- Do you understand the idea of *salaam*—peace—in Muslim thinking and how it relates to the peace we can have with God through Christ? Try explaining it to a friend using Romans 5 v 1-2. Which ideas in these verses will be especially difficult or attractive for a Muslim to hear?

- Do you think you would be comfortable with, or capable of, sharing the gospel from the *Qur'an*?

- How easy will you find it to talk about the way the Lord is *intimately* involved in your life? Is there a challenge here for your own walk with God?

Working with Muslim families — some do's and don'ts

What you should do:

1. **Research and find the Muslim neighborhoods in your area.** Find ways to interface with local residents through volunteering at centers that offer free food, diapers, clothing, tutoring or English classes.

2. **Ladies, don't be afraid to sit down next to Muslim mothers who are in the park with their children.** Start talking about the children and engage them in conversation. Set up another day to meet there and bring a few refreshments to share. Ask for their phone number and send them a few simple encouraging texts or a funny picture before your next meeting. Ask lots of questions. Discover what their needs are and volunteer to help. You may very well end up taking them to the doctor, helping them understand a letter they received in the mail, explaining how to do some of their children's homework. Ask questions about how they spend their time. If they confess to being lonely, invite them over for a cup of tea and a play date with the children. Ask them if they have friends outside of their culture and volunteer to be one.

3. **Do ask Muslim women you meet if they know anyone who needs help with conversational English** and offer to go to their home or meet them at a café.

4. **Women should feel free to approach Muslim women who are older or younger than you.** Typically they are pleased to make a friend of any age. If they do not have extended family nearby, they will be very excited to spend time with women the same age as their mother, grandmother, sister or aunt. It meets a need and fills a loss. If you give their children permission to call you auntie or grandma, they will be very honored.

5. **Do spend time with Muslim women in their home or yours.** They will be more comfortable than if you meet at a café or restaurant.

6. **Always take your shoes off when you enter a Muslim home, even when they tell you not to.** Men, when you enter the house, make sure your friend's wife has had time to cover her head with a scarf, if that is her custom.

7. **Do reach out to the whole family.** If a Muslim family begins to follow Christ, as opposed to an individual, they have a built-in support system when word gets out and persecution begins. After contact has been made and a friendship started with a member of the same sex, every effort should be made by your family to meet the rest of the family and establish relationships with everyone, so that husbands are reaching husbands and wives sharing with wives. Remember that *families reach families*; make that a priority in your strategy.

8. **When you enter a room full of Muslims, men should go around and shake every other man's hand.** Females should shake hands with or kiss on the cheek every female present. Greetings are important.

9. **When you are invited to a Muslim home, take a box of cookies or candy, nuts, some juice or sodas.** Even a very small gesture is noted and appreciated.

10. **Interact with and love their children but do not try to evangelize them.** It will be the end of your relationship. Share your faith with the parents; the children will hear and absorb. Maybe they will be the first in the family to come to Christ when they are adults.

11. **When you have a relationship with a Muslim family, they will see how you raise your children and will soon be asking you for advice.** That advice can lead to sharing biblical principles and to very good discussions.

12. **If you are invited by your Muslim friends to celebrate a religious holiday, birthday, wedding or other special event, go and expect to spend several hours.** Remember presence is important. Sometimes there are no opportunities to share faith at these events but new relationships are made and opportunities arise for very meaningful conversations.

13. **Every time they share a need or problem, ask them if you can pray for them and do it immediately in the name of Jesus.** When issues are resolved, remind them that it was through Jesus the Messiah—who has power over evil spirits, nature, health, and death—that their prayer was answered.

14. **Do ask questions about their faith to initiate dialogue and ask if you can share what you believe.** If you are discussing issues related to being a woman, share stories about how God provided food for women in need (Elijah and the widow), children for those who are barren (Hannah and Sarah), safety and protection for Abigail, presence and guidance for Hagar, healing for the woman with an issue of blood, life to a little girl and a widow's only son.

15. **Do take flowers to the hospital if they have a baby and a gift for the baby after they are home.**

16. **Do rejoice if they tell you they are having dreams about God or Jesus speaking to them.** If you can relate what is being said in the dreams to a Bible verse or story, don't hesitate to share it with them. Follow up with them about how God is working in their life.

What you should not do:

1. **Never stop visiting a Muslim friend if it is awkward at first or there are long awkward pauses.** Often they have the television on, so watch it a little; then when you think of something else to discuss, go at it again. Play with the children. Be a learner and ask lots of questions about their country, religion, culture and food. If you are a woman, ask them how to make one of their traditional dishes. If you are a man, talk to them about "*futbal*" (Soccer in the American context); most of the men love sports.

2. **Do not shake hands with the opposite sex unless they offer a hand first.**

3. **Don't become disheartened when they tell you the Bible is corrupted.** Be prepared to tell them what the Qur'an says about the Bible and how we have Biblical texts dating from times before the Qur'an was written. Refer to the resources on page 111 to help you with these types of disagreements. Mostly be consistent and honest as you discuss these issues. Don't take offense and try not to give offense.

4. **Don't be surprised when you invite a Muslim friend to go somewhere and she always, no matter what the occasion, has her kids in tow.** She has total responsibility for the children, and even if the father is home, he will often expect her to take them with her.

5. **Don't tell a Muslim friend about another seeker who is asking questions, studying the Bible, attending church or has made a profession of faith.** This can result in persecution for the one seeking. Only that seeker has the right to share with others.

6. **Don't become disillusioned if you find out that something they told you is not true.** Lying is okay in their assessment if it prevents shame or embarrassment. Remember, you are working with people from a shame-and-honor society.

7. **Don't expect Muslim women to have high self-esteem or confidence.** Some will, but in a Muslim court of law it takes two women's testimonies to equal that of a man. In many Muslim countries she has few rights, even regarding her children, and the sons are always valued more than daughters. Her future is often decided for her—even who she will marry.

8. **Don't be taken aback when your Muslim friend is very possessive and wants you to be best friends with him or her only**. There is not always a lot of trust between people outside of the family, so fewer friends are better in their estimation.

9. **Don't be discouraged when they say "no" to Christ, even when you know he is dealing with them.** They are afraid. The repercussions are very great. Let them count the cost in their own time and in their own way.

Fatima's story

Fatima grew up in a difficult family to say the least. She was never allowed to attend school, always had to work around the house, and was subject to verbal and physical abuse by her brothers and other family members. When she was old enough, she escaped to Europe, where she thought she would be safe.

Since she had never been to school, Fatima had never learned to read or write. Now she was living in a country where she couldn't speak the language very well, where she didn't have legal residency and had no family to help her. She was able to find some jobs cleaning houses, but that didn't pay well, so it wasn't long before she turned to prostitution. It wasn't something she wanted to do; she knew it was wrong but it paid the bills and enabled her to stay in the country and not return home.

Soon she met a man who took her in, and once again she knew it was wrong to live with him without being married—but because of her legal status there was no simple way to marry him. She soon had two children, both boys, but by then her "husband" had gone back to his old ways and was abusing drugs and sometimes her. Her children were nationals of the country she was living in because her "husband" had signed the birth certificates, but she was still un-documented. She knew she needed to leave him, but it was difficult since he provided her and her children with a home where she was relatively safe.

It was then that she met some followers of Jesus. She started working for them and they welcomed her, not as a servant in their home but as a friend who worked for them. They treated her with respect and paid her an honest wage. They even helped her with the children from time to time and started trying to help her get legal status. But there was more; they also started telling her stories of *Isa*—Jesus.

These stories were unlike anything she had heard before. These stories were true, Fatima could tell. It wasn't long before she met some women from her former country who were now followers of Jesus. She couldn't believe it, and she couldn't get the stories out of her mind. She also couldn't deny how these followers of Jesus were so different from everyone else she met.

So she started going to their Bible study. They told more stories of Jesus and other stories from the *Torah*. These stories were so different. This Jesus was not who she expected. In the end, she had no choice—she knew she had to follow him too. Just like the other women, she couldn't resist any longer. She made a choice and decided to follow Jesus.

Chapter five

Bible passages to share with Muslims

Muslims are told that the Bible has been corrupted. In practice, though, most Muslims are happy to hear, read and discuss stories from the Bible. We have found that telling biblical stories is the most effective way to start conversations.

The person who you are speaking to will determine if you just tell a story or if you open God's word and have them read directly from the text and do Bible study with you. If they are able to read English, encourage them to look at the story with you from the Bible. If they are unable to read, or if you feel they would find an open Bible too intimidating, then simply tell them the story. Either will work—the point is to get them hearing the word of

God, because "faith comes from hearing the message, and the message is heard through the word about Christ" (Romans 10 v 17).

Let me give you an example. When we were working overseas, one of the first stories we would tell was the Good Samaritan. We might not tell them this is a story told by Jesus; it all depended on how well we knew them. We would tell the story and then talk about what it means to love your neighbor and who your neighbor is.

This story, like many others in the Gospels, is startling news for a Muslim. It completely contradicts the Islamic paradigm of subjugating your neighbor and encourages us to show them love instead. Our new friends would discuss this story for weeks at a time, trying to understand all its implications. Eventually we would tell them that this was a teaching of Jesus and take them to God's word.

Remember, they may know many of these stories as well—but have a different version. If they interrupt, tell them you want to tell or read with them the story from the biblical text first, and then they can tell their version. This is sometimes called "situational Bible storying", which can be done anywhere and at any time. Just bring the Bible story into your conversation wherever you are. Because story telling is a strong feature of Muslim culture it will not seem odd to them.

One Christian I know will get under the radar by putting Bible stories into a Muslim setting. He tells Jesus' story about the tax collector and the pharisee like this:

There was once a thief and an imam who went to the mosque to pray. The imam prayed: "I thank you

God that I read the scriptures, I have been on the Hajj, I pray five times a day, and give alms. I thank you that I am not like this wretched thief". The thief simply bowed before God and said "Have mercy on me, a sinner".

He then asks his friends: *"Which one do you think Allah will accept into heaven?"* Almost universally, they say: *"The imam of course!"*. In reply he tells them: *"your prophet Jesus says it is the thief..."*. It is always guaranteed to start an interesting conversation about what makes us right with God.

From the beginning

There are many stories like this you can share, but eventually you want to start from the beginning, so that you can explain the whole of the gospel message. This story list is short and as you get to know your friends and their worldview, you will want to adjust and add stories that you think will find traction in their minds and lives. The good news is you *can't go wrong* telling Bible stories and studying God's word with your Muslim friend. God has promised:

> ... so is my word that goes out from my mouth: It will not return to me empty, but will accomplish what I desire and achieve the purpose for which I sent it.
> *Isaiah 55 v 11*

We have found the stories below to be particularly helpful in sharing the gospel with Muslims, and to lead to fruitful conversation and discussion.

Genesis 1 – 2

Start with creation: one God, Creator of everything. As you tell or read the story, help your friend see the intimate nature of God. When you talk about the creation of Adam and Eve, use the Genesis 2 account, as it demonstrates great love and care on the part of God. God makes man from the dust of the earth and then breathes life into him. Then after Adam names all the animals, and finds no suitable helper (Genesis 2 v 20), God puts Adam to sleep and takes a rib from his side. The picture is of a God who loves, is concerned with and enjoys his creation. Remember, God is distant in Islam; in the Bible's creation God is near!

Points to ponder:

- One God, Creator and Sustainer of the universe.
- The intimate nature of God.

Genesis 3

After you have dealt with creation, move on to the fall. In the fall you want to emphasize the magnitude of a very simple sin. The Islamic mind thinks of sin only as acts seen by others which bring shame to the family—adultery, murder, stealing, things you go to jail for. Adam and Eve ate fruit from a tree! They disobeyed the holy God and for that they were banished from the presence of God. Emphasize the consequences of sin: separation from God, the judgment of God on creation, the judgment of God on the relationship between men and women, the shame of sin and our inability to make things right. Conclude the story with God killing an animal, shedding blood, to cover Adam and Eve.

Points to ponder
- Sin is anything that dishonors God.
- God is just and must punish sin.
- Blood was shed as a result of Adam and Eve's sin.

Genesis 4

Cain and Abel come next. Tell the story and then help them see that Cain's sacrifice was not acceptable because it was not what God wanted. Abel shed the blood of an animal, and that blood is necessary for the forgiveness of sins. You want to bring out this theme with your Muslim friends so when you get to Jesus, they have an understanding of why he would die on the cross and shed his blood for the forgiveness of our sins.

Points to ponder
- God has expectations for our worship and our lives; we cannot do what we want; we must meet His expectations.
- The shedding of blood is necessary for forgiveness.

I hope you are getting the idea. Pick your stories from throughout the Bible, placing emphasis on the following:

1. Intimacy with God; God cares for the individual
- Genesis 12: the personal call of God to Abraham
- Genesis 16: God speaks to Hagar

2. Sin is a violation of relationship with God and it will be punished
- Genesis 7: the flood
- Genesis 11: the Tower of Babel

3. Sacrifice is necessary for the forgiveness of sins

- Leviticus 16 v 11-22: This passage is a little harder than others but what you are sharing is that there was a requirement for the shedding of blood for forgiveness of sins. There was a whole process that the priest and the people had to follow because sin against God is a serious thing.
- Genesis 22: The offering of Isaac as a sacrifice and the substitution of a lamb.
- Matthew 26-28: Eventually you will share the story of Jesus' death and resurrection. I recommend taking time before you get there so that you have built a good background and your friend can understand sacrifice clearly.

4. A relationship with God is based on repentance and forgiveness

- Psalm 32, 51 and 2 Samuel 11 – 12: These stories and Bible passages can really impact a Muslim. Many Muslims will suggest that the prophets like David were without sin. Islamic teaching is hard to understand on this point. Surah 47:19 indicates that Muhammad was to ask God for forgiveness. At the same time there is a general understanding that all the prophets enjoyed *"isma"*—protection—against sin. Psalm 51 is powerful because it says that David sinned and his sin was against God, even though the story in 2 Samuel shows us his sin was against Bathsheba and Uriah. So sin is something we do against God, and everyone sins—except Jesus.

5. *Jesus calls us to a deep and life-changing response*

- Matthew 5 – 6: Read through the Sermon on the Mount and discuss it in small sections with your friend. I have known many Muslims come to faith as a result of reading the Sermon on the Mount. Jesus' teaching about anger, murder, adultery, forgiveness, the heart and many other things, runs completely against the thinking and culture of Islam.

- The parables, teachings and stories of Jesus: Jesus told the parables and preached his sermons in a way that greatly impacted an Eastern mindset— much like that of your Muslim friend. I have regularly been surprised that my friends respond to these stories in ways I have never thought of. The word of God is truly powerful!

This list is just an example of some of the stories and Bible passages to be read or retold to your Muslim friend. It is nothing more than a starter list. Tell the stories that are important to you; mostly just get into God's word with your friend.

Aisha's story

I was invited to take part in a course called *Discovering Jesus Through Asian Eyes* at a church near where I live. I am from a Muslim family, but there were two other girls from a Hindu background who were also interested in Christianity.

The course answered a lot of questions that the majority of Asians ask about Jesus and faith in God. It was very relaxed and enjoyable as we talked about these questions and looked at passages in the Bible. What amazed me was to discover that believing in Jesus is very different from the rules and beliefs that I had tried to follow.

It became evident that many of my "beliefs" were based more around culture and man-made rules. For me, having clear words from God from the Bible strengthened my belief that there is a living God.

As each session went by, I realized that I didn't have to change who I was—my Bengali culture, my relationships, my clothing, or the food I liked—to be a follower of Jesus Christ. All I needed to do was claim Jesus as my Savior. I could be the same person for my family and for myself.

I have never felt such peace in God. Now I know the Holy Spirit is guiding me, giving me peace, wisdom and courage—and I just feel so loved. I don't feel lonely anymore.

Chapter six

Reaching out as a church

I have spent a lot of time talking about what you can do one on one with Muslims, especially new immigrants, but what are some ways in which your church as a whole can start to reach out to Muslims?

There are many opportunities to bring the *salaam* of the gospel to them. One of the first things you want to think through is how you can teach and encourage the members of your congregation to love those who are different from themselves.

Sadly, Muslims have become the focus of suspicion for many people in the wider population. This is something that Muslims feel deeply, and which encourages them to maintain close, exclusive communities. It is easy for this mentality to invade our thinking as believers too, because the truth is we like to congregate with those who are most like us.

So encourage your pastor to preach and teach on the subject of loving your neighbor. There is no clearer text for today then the story of the Good Samaritan. Although the cultural gulf between us may be as large as that between the Samaritan and the injured man, Jesus taught us to love our neighbor with practical care and sacrificial service.

Immigrant Muslims have been taught that in coming to a foreign country they are now in *dar al-harb* (the house of war). They have lived in *dar al-islam* (the house of Islam) but now they have moved to a new place, with a new culture and a new way of living. Many are going through culture shock and need attention and love.

Receive different cultures

The first thing your church needs to do is learn to receive different cultures in its building. When a lost person comes inside our building, we cannot expect them to act like a Christian. When a Muslim enters your building, you cannot expect them to act like a Christian. The women may wear head scarves; they feel naked without them. We have no cause to feel threatened by this.

They will not eat pork and they will be uncomfortable if they think the meat served as part of the food on offer is not *halal* (that is, meat butchered by a Muslim). There are many things they can and will eat, but don't ask them to change if they are not yet followers of Jesus.

Find ways to get them into your building, around believers that you have trained and taught. When the average Muslim comes into a Christian church, they are not sure what to expect. When they find love, acceptance and concern for their well-being, when they find their children being loved and taught good morals and truths, then they will love you and become all the more receptive to the gospel.

English language classes

One easy way to get them relating with believers, and perhaps inside your building, is through holding formal or informal language classes—this will be especially appropriate for newly arrived immigrants. At my church we have a full-blown English as a New Language (ENL) program, and on any given week you will find 30 to 40 Iraqis, fully scarved and covered, wandering our halls. The children are attending our children's programs, and the parents are learning English from followers of Jesus who love them, and often demonstrate concern for them by going to their homes and helping them through issues they have as they adjust to the West.

If your congregation can talk, then they can teach their language. All anyone needs are materials, a heart for teaching, and the ability to form words. Train your members to be good ENL teachers. You should be able to find someone either in your church or close by who can train your volunteers. We have been blessed with several excellent ENL teachers who have trained our volunteers. It is a beautiful thing to come to church on Wednesday nights and see the nations represented. It is a beautiful thing to come to church and see people who need Jesus inside the building. What better place to find Jesus than inside the church doors!

When you start this ministry, it will not be easy. Some of the children, especially the babies, have never been without their mothers. The first few weeks are fairly traumatic for the kids and the childcare workers; however, the mothers are usually pretty excited to have someone else care for their children. It helps if you can get the childcare workers to the homes of the immigrants so the kids begin to see them in other places besides the church. Adjustment will come quicker when they are with them in their safe place: their homes. Not everyone in your church will like this either. You will just have to find ways to confront bad attitudes and help people see the gospel in action!

Most churches run mother and baby or toddler groups. Again, this is a potentially fertile area of contact as many mothers with small children feel very isolated and lonely. Make sure that you advertize the existence of your groups in places where Muslims will see it—for example, in shop windows in areas where people congregate. The friendship and contact with Christians at these kind of groups will break down barriers and build a bridge for the gospel.

Tutoring

A second important ministry a church can get involved in is tutoring programs for children, and conversational English for women or couples in their homes. We often think that children just pick up languages without any work. Not true! Children have to work at language and it does not always come easily. For first generation immigrants, this will be a massive help.

Find tutors who are prepared to go into homes to work with the kids on their homework. If the tutor is a lady, make sure the mother is there; if the tutor is a man, make sure the father is there. Don't cross the lines. If only the mother is at home, then a male tutor should come at a different time or tutor in a public place. If only the father is there, then the same applies for the female tutor.

Conversational English is a great inroad to friendship with a family as well. I know a family where the husband and wife do this ministry together. Every Saturday you can find them in the home of a new immigrant family, helping them with their English. Over time, a real friendship has developed and they have brought their new friends to church. They are slowly sharing the truth of the gospel with them in a wonderful way

Respect is important—adapt to their culture; don't ask them to adapt to yours. While the tutor is there, they will be asked to help with lots of other issues—what a great way to make friends!

Persecution

Lastly, there will be persecution—not typically against you, but persecution will happen to your Muslim friend. Mothers will be ridiculed for going into the church and allowing their children to learn Bible verses. Sometimes as the family starts coming closer to understanding who Jesus is, Satan will step up the attacks and the family will be ostracized by their community.

Because they are in the West, they are less likely to be harmed physically, but there have been cases when a college student or single person disappears—normally having been returned to their home country. There have also been cases where the *imam* from the family village has called the immigrant and told them they were endangering their family in their home country. They have been told to leave the Christians, and sometimes to move to a new city so their family back home would be protected.

Don't treat persecution lightly: being ostracized is very difficult, so you will need to be a new family for this family. Threats should be taken seriously. As a family is going through this, help them figure out what they should do. Sometimes they may need to move to another area so they are not around the Muslims threatening their family. Find ways to help them.

Some suggest that ENL should not be done in a church for this reason. There are people groups and places where that might be the case, so obviously you will have to work on a case-by-case basis. I like having ENL in the church because it introduces the learners to other believers. However, you will need to evaluate how it is going. We find if we teach ENL and do a good job, the problems are lessened. If what we are doing is solely trying to evangelize while they are in our church building, but not doing a good job with ENL, then problems accelerate. If you demonstrate that you are making a difference in people's lives, then your friends will have a great reason to be there.

There are many other programs your church can offer: sports programs, special meals—almost anything that gets Muslims across the threshold of your doors. The goal is for them to experience real community and genuine Christian love, and develop relationships with Christians who will love and befriend them. All of these events are nothing more than starting points for relationships that will get followers of Jesus into homes where real friendships can begin. Never forget it is all about loving your neighbor as Jesus so clearly taught us.

Conclusion

The goal of this book has been to introduce you to Islam and give you some ideas and techniques for sharing your faith with your Muslim neighbor and friend. My desire is that you take these ideas and grow them, find what works, share your life and share Jesus with your Muslim friend. Jesus is the only hope your friend has for finding peace; I pray that he or she finds peace because you cared enough to share.

Resources
Books to help you understand

A Christian's pocket guide to Islam *Malcolm Steer*, Christian Focus, 2003

The Crescent through the Eyes of the Cross: Insights from an Arab Christian *Nabeel Jabbour,* NavPress, 2008

The Emergence of Islam: Classical Traditions in Contemporary Perspective *Gabriel Said Reynolds*, Fortress Press, 2012.
Note: *This is not a Christian book but it is solid.*

Answering Islam: The Crescent in Light of the Cross *Norman Geisler and Abdul Saleeb*, Baker, 2002

What every Christian needs to know about the Qur'an *James R White*, Bethany House Publishers, 2013

Breaking the Islam Code: Understanding the Soul Questions of Every Muslim *J D Greear*, Harvest House Publishers, 2010

Books to help you engage and communicate

Seeking Allah, finding Jesus *Nabeel Qureshi*, Zondervan, 2014

Ex-Muslim: how one daring prayer to Jesus changed a life forever. *Naeem Fazal,* Thomas Nelson, 2014

The Gospel for Muslims: An Encouragement to Share Christ with Confidence, *Thabiti Anyabwile*, Moody, 2012

Daughters of Islam: Building Bridges with Muslim Women *Miriam Adeney*, Intervarsity Press, 2002

Ministry to Muslim Women: Longing to call them Sisters *Fran Love and Jeleta Eckhart (editors)*, William Carey Library, 2003

From Fear to Faith: Muslim and Christian Women *Karol Downey & Mary Ann Cate*, William Carey Library, 2003

Miniskirts, Mothers and Muslims: A Christian Woman in a Muslim Land, *Christine A. Mallouhi*, Monarch Books, 2004

Books to lend or give to Muslims

Any of the Gospels! Luke is useful as its opening establishes the historical credibility of the book—something that Muslims may dispute.

The Torn Veil *Esther Gulshan*, Brown and Co., 2004

I Dared to Call Him Father: The Miraculous Story of a Muslim Woman's Encounter with God *Bilquis Sheikh*, Baker, 2003

Other evangelistic resources

The Word of Life Bible Correspondence Course
(UK and Australia)
www.word.org.uk/course
www.word.org.au/course

Jesus through Asian Eyes
This is an evangelistic booklet and study course that gently shares the gospel with Asians of all religions and backgrounds. Its themes touch on many areas that Muslims have concerns about. Further details on pages 117-119

Christianity Explored
This is an evangelistic course that takes people through the Gospel of Mark. The website has many testimonies and answers to common questions about the Christian faith.
www.christianityexplored.org

Christianity Explained
Similar structure to the above, but designed to be used one to one.
www.thegoodbook.com

The World We All Want
A Bible-overview approach to telling the gospel story. This seven-part course has much more Old Testament in it than many other evangelistic studies, so may be more appropriate for some Muslims.
www.thegoodbook.com

Organizations

There are many wonderful organizations that promote and offer training and resources for outreach work with Muslims. Their websites are encouraging, and many of them have helpful testimonies and other resources.

- **MECO – Middle East Christian Outreach**

- **the Gospel for Muslims**

- **Arab World Ministries-Pioneers**

- **Frontiers**

- **i2 Ministries**

- **The Jenkins Center** *www.jenkins.sbts.edu*

- **Ravi Zacharias International Ministries.** Dr. Nabeel Qureshi is a former devout Muslim who was convinced of the truth of Christianity through historical reasoning and a spiritual search for God. Since his conversion, he has dedicated his life to spreading the Gospel.

Websites

IsaalMashih:
isaalmasih.net
is a website for Muslims that explains the gospel from a Muslim's perspective, and answers many objections and questions which they may have.

Answering Islam:
www.answering-islam.org
A multi-language website that offers many perspectives in the form of a dialogue between Christians and Muslims. Some good articles here to form the basis of a discussion with a Muslim friend.

The People of the book:
thepeopleofthebook.org
Has lots of videos and background to reaching out to Muslims.

Answering Muslims:
www.answeringmuslims. com There is a particularly extensive section on women in Islam on this website.

Debate

www.debate.org.uk
Contains lots of video material that might be useful for pointing an interested Muslim toward.

4truth

www.4truth.net
Good information on lots of other world religions and sects. Good site for simple research.

WWITV

www.wwitv.com
This looks like sat7 on the internet. It has some good and some not so good programming—so be discerning!

Light of Life

www.light-of-life.com
This website contains books in English and Arabic. Some are direct translations of Islamic texts clarifying issues such as apostasy from an Islamic viewpoint. It also has some excellent resources for your Muslim friend.

St. Francis Magazine

www.stfrancismagazine.info
St Francis Magazine is a publication of Arab Vision and Interserve. Both organizations are committed to witnessing to Jesus Christ in the Arab world. *St Francis Magazine* aims to strengthen the Christian witness in the Arab World.

Ministering to Muslims

www.ministeringtomuslims. com
This site has a number of valuable resources for both the person sharing the gospel with Muslims and for Muslims to read and understand for themselves.

Arabic Bible Outreach

www.arabicbible.com
Arabic Bible Outreach Ministry is a Christian mission organization with a passion to extend the word of God to the Arab and Muslim world. Its vision is to see vibrant and reproducing churches in the Arab world and among large Muslim communities in North America.

Films:

www.godsstories.ae
In English and Arabic this
site presents a series of Old
Testament stories in film
format. They can be watched
either in their entirety or in
sections with Nizar Shaheen
narrating the stories. All in
Arabic, filmed with Middle-
Eastern actors, the full-
length films have subtitles in
English.

Jesus Film

www.jesusfilmmedia.org
Watch the *Jesus* film in the
language of your choice.

Introducing an exciting new
outreach resource

Discovering
Jesus
through Asian eyes

Discovering

Jesus

through Asian eyes

What's the opportunity?

Millions of people with an Asian background live in the West. Some have only recently arrived; others have lived in the West for many generations. Asians are often more open to talking about spiritual things than many longer-established residents.

How can one resource speak to such a diverse group of people?

It might seem strange to create a set of resources that tries to speak to people with such a diverse range of beliefs and cultures. What could be more different than Buddhism and Islam? What do Japanese people and Bangladeshis have in common?

But Asians of all kinds share many attitudes in common: an openness to talking about spiritual things; a feeling that they must live up to family expectations; a sense of honor. But most of all, they share the view that Christianity is a Western religion.

The outreach booklet and course pick up on these common cultural ways of thinking to present the good news about Jesus in a way that is open, friendly and appealing.

What is the *Jesus through Asian eyes* booklet?

This full-color booklet is designed to be given to Asians of any background. It asks and answers 16 of the most frequently asked questions that people have about Jesus, Christianity and faith in God. It is filled with warm testimonies from Asian people from all kinds of backgrounds who have discovered the love of God in Christ.

The questions are answered carefully from the Bible in a way that is culturally sensitive and gently leads the reader toward belief in Jesus. The booklet is designed to be given to anyone from an Asian background—a neighbor, friend or colleague from work.

How does the course work?

The *Discovering Jesus through Asian eyes* course is based on the booklet. If someone has read the booklet and wants to know more, you can invite them to join you to explore the questions in a little more depth. The course is split into eight sessions; each looks at two questions from the booklet. The emphasis is on friendly, open discussions which examine passages from the Bible. The studies have been extensively trialed and tested with a wide variety of Middle Eastern and Asian people.

What materials are available?

- The *Jesus through Asian eyes* booklet is a beautifully designed and produced 32-page colorful publication. You can buy it for a much reduced price when you purchase in bulk.

- The *Leader's Guide* contains everything you need to know to run a course—extensive notes on the discussion questions, helpful advice on how to address issues relevant to different people groups and religions, and ideas for promoting the course and conducting outreach to Asians in your local area.

- The *Discussion Guide* is for each person who attends a course. It contains questions and Bible passages, plus testimonies and explanations of difficult terms.

- Dedicated website at **www.discovering-jesus.com**

- Promotional flyers and posters available.

- More information at **www.thegoodbook.com**

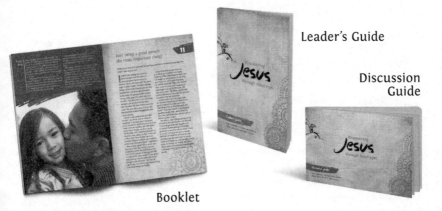

Leader's Guide

Discussion Guide

Booklet

Other titles in this series

Engaging with Hindus
by Robin Thomson

Hinduism is the third largest faith in the world, and yet many Christians know very little about Hindu beliefs and lifestyle

This short book is designed to help both Christians and whole churches understand more about Hindus, and to reach out to them with the good news of the gospel.

Robin Thomson spent twenty years in India teaching the Bible and training church leaders. He is the author of several books relating the Bible to Asian culture.

Engaging with Atheists
by David Robertson

Many Christians are fearful of engaging in conversation with atheists—believing that they will be hostile to Christian beliefs and conversations about the Bible.

This short book is designed to help both Christians and whole churches understand more about the questions and issues that atheists of various kinds have about Christian faith, and to reach out to them with the good news of the gospel.

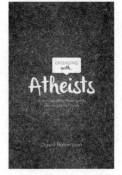

David Robertson is the minister of St Peter's Free Church in Dundee, Scotland, and a director of the Solas Centre for Public Christianity. He is the author of The Dawkins Letters, and has publicly debated Richard Dawkins and other prominent atheists throughout the UK and Europe.

Order from your local Good Book website:
North America: www.thegoodbook.com
UK & Europe: www.thegoodbook.co.uk
Australia: www.thegoodbook.com.au
New Zealand: www.thegoodbook.co.nz

An excellent series for building your own faith, and helping others discover the Christian message for themselves

How can I be sure?

by John Stevens

Many Christians experience times of doubt and uncertainty. At various times we can ask: Does God love me? Am I really a Christian?— and even—Is there a God at all?!

This short, readable book unpacks the difference between good and bad doubt; and shows us where it comes from and how to deal with it in ourselves and others. It explains clearly and simply the liberating reality of what the Bible tells us about doubt, assurance and the Christian life.

What happens when I die?

by Marcus Nodder

We all have questions about death. Despite the strong assurance the Bible gives us about life beyond the grave, Christians are often troubled by other questions. What will happen on the day of judgment? Will we have bodies in heaven? Will there be rewards?

These short, simple books are designed to help Christians understand what God has said about these questions in the Scriptures.

Order from your local Good Book website:
North America: www.thegoodbook.com
UK & Europe: www.thegoodbook.co.uk
Australia: www.thegoodbook.com.au
New Zealand: www.thegoodbook.co.nz

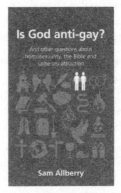

thegoodbook
COMPANY

Opening up the Bible

At The Good Book Company, we are dedicated to helping Christians and local churches grow. We believe that God's growth process always starts with hearing clearly what He has said to us through His timeless word—the Bible.

Ever since we opened our doors in 1991, we have been striving to produce resources that honor God in the way the Bible is used. We have grown to become an international provider of user-friendly resources to the Christian community, with believers of all backgrounds and denominations using our Bible studies, books, evangelistic resources, DVD-based courses and training events.

We want to equip ordinary Christians to live for Christ day by day, and churches to grow in their knowledge of God, their love for one another, and the effectiveness of their outreach.

Call us for a discussion of your needs or visit one of our local websites for more information on the resources and services we provide.

North America: www.thegoodbook.com
UK & Europe: www.thegoodbook.co.uk
Australia: www.thegoodbook.com.au
New Zealand: www.thegoodbook.co.nz

North America: 866 244 2165
UK & Europe: 0333 123 0880
Australia: (02) 6100 4211
New Zealand (+64) 3 343 1990